PARSONS'

GENERAL THEORY OF ACTION

A Summary of The Basic Theory

by

B. J. Bluth, Ph. D

Granada Hills, California
1982

PARSONS' GENERAL THEORY OF ACTION: A SUMMARY OF THE BASIC THEORY

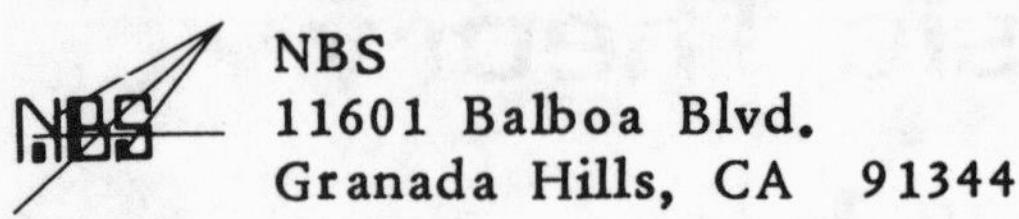

NBS
11601 Balboa Blvd.
Granada Hills, CA 91344

Library of Congress Cataloging in Publication Data

Bluth, B.J., 1934-
Parsons' general theory of action.

Bibliography: p.
1. Social Action. I. Title.
HM24.B56 301.01 82-3408
ISBN 0-937654-02-7 AACR2

Cover Design by Randy Thomson

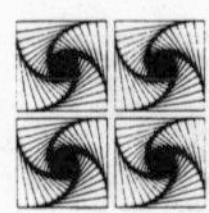

TABLE OF CONTENTS

1

OVERVIEW OF THE GENERAL THEORY OF ACTION

"If it is the present we wish to understand, then it is above all with Talcott Parsons that we must be concerned". Alvin Gouldner

There is little argument that Talcott Parsons' General Theory of Action is an important influencing factor in the work of many sociologists and political scientists, and has been for many years. However, the task of extracting the theory from its primary sources is formidable, and far beyond the available time of many interested students and scholars. The total development of the General Theory of Action spreads over some fifty years and is found, part by part, in over one hundred and seventy books and articles published since 1928. Unfortunately, there is no one single book in which Professor Parsons has attempted to present a complete and systematic explanation of the whole theory that would be suited to the undergraduate reader, and this book attempts to fill that gap.

Most of the work of Talcott Parsons can be separated into two major categories: general theory and application essays. The application essays analyze many different situations and events, such as full citizenship for the American Negro, Christianity and modern industrial society, as well as problems of the professions, economics, sex roles, etc. Usually the theoretical assumptions and underlying frames of reference are not explained in the essays, but nevertheless, the whole of the General Theory of Action acts as the unstated assumption. While developing the theory itself, Parsons often concentrates on one area and set of ideas, with the in-depth development of other ideas in separate books or articles. Thus those reading Parsons' work for the first time often find it quite difficult.

This book is intended to introduce you to the basic skeletal set of concepts of the General Theory of Action in a coherent presentation. It is not intended to be a substitute, nor is it supposed to be complete. It is a "starter" book, written to help you begin reading the essays, the theory itself, or the many criticisms of Parsons' work. There are many other concepts, aspects, and developments that are not included. To get a full grasp of the theory and the richness of Professor Parsons elaboration of it, you really need to read some of the original articles and books that Professor Parsons wrote, and to help you do that, suggestions are given in the section on "Supplemental Readings" in the Appendix.

Studying the General Theory of Action is like watching someone draw. No matter how or where they start, you don't know what the picture means until it is finished. Although there are only a few major elements to the theory, no one aspect makes complete sense alone or disconnected from the rest. It is necessary to see the total configuration as a whole. It also helps to realize that the "aspects" are not "parts" or separate entities just added together. Each element of the General Theory of Action is but a different view or perspective, separate because it is only a alternate view, not because it represents a distinctive reality. For example, you cannot understand statistical averages separate from multiplication, addition, or the use of numbers. To be able to do statistics requires mastery of the other basic mathematical characters and processes. Thus, it is important to remember, as you are working through this material, that the General Theory of Action only makes sense in its interconnectedness, and that only comes once you have completed the whole round of the discussion. Once you have finished reading through the book the first time, it is recommended you read it again to fully appreciate the way all the parts of the theory fit together.

I. FIVE ASPECTS OF THE GENERAL THEORY OF ACTION

The five aspects of the General Theory of Action are:

1. The nature of theory and science
2. The Elements of Action
3. Systems of Action
4. Sub-systems of the System of Action
5. The Pattern Variables

A. ASSUMPTIONS:

Sections 1 and 2 constitute the assumptions of the General Theory of Action. Parsons' idea about what a theory is and how it relates to science is especially important in that it is not universally held in the social sciences. Thus he uses terms and vocabulary that are common to social science, but because his assumptions are different, he effectively transforms those concepts into something quite distinctive. The result can be very confusing if you are not aware of the change in perspective. It is comparable to the ways you could interpret the statement, "he hung himself". One way is the idea that the person actually committed suicide and is now dead. The other is a figure of speech used to imply that someone got into trouble by what he said. He gave himself away. It makes a lot of difference.

Section 2, The Elements of Action, introduces the set of assumptions of the General Theory of Action. Here Parsons defines some of the basic positions he takes about the character of action and actors in situations. However, because these concepts do not lend themselves easily to verification, or because they are so complex in relation to actual events, they do not become constituent elements of the General Theory of Action itself. They act as an important point of departure into the facets of the theory itself, which is derived from the Elements of Action.

B. SYSTEMS OF ACTION:

The body of the General Theory of Action, Sections 3, 4 and 5, is composed of three ideas: Sub-systems of Action which are composed of Culture Systems, Social Systems, and Personality Systems; the System of Action itself made-up of the four elements of all action systems, namely Adaptive, Goal Attainment, Integration, and Latent Pattern Maintenance; and finally, the Pattern Variables which are the primary connecting link between all levels of the General Theory of Action, as well as the major tool used to relate the theory to events. The whole of the General Theory of Action is represented in Plate I. (These Plates are designed to be folded-out for easy reference during the entire discussion of a section.)

Finally, a word is necessary about the lack of direct quotations from Parsons' himself. Most of the ideas in the General Theory of Action are parts of complex loops of ideas that are long and difficult because of the specialized language used. Thus, without extremely long quotations, the ideas lose their meaning and can be easily misinterpreted out of their context. An attempt is made to relate the ideas discussed here with some of Parsons' original writings in the Appendix. Also, there will be no attempt in this book to provide any critical evaluation of the General Theory of Action. Ample criticism is widely available in the sociological literature, both positive and negative.

II. THE FOLD-OUT PLATES

At the end of the book are nine Plates that are designed to be folded out so you can look at them the entire time you are reading the section devoted to the development of the ideas included. This should make it easier to follow the discussion as it relates to the concepts presented in the diagram.

2

THE THEORETICAL ORIENTATION

The hardest thing to remember about the General Theory of Action is that it is **NOT** a theory of "action," but that it is a THEORY of action. It is a device, a language, a set of ideas to be used in understanding and predicting events. It is not a replica of the events of everyday life. As Goethe put it in Faust, "All theory, dear friend, is grey, but the Golden Tree of actual life springs ever green."

Understanding this point of view of the General Theory of Action is made more difficult by the fact that Parsons defines terms and words with his own meanings. At times, these meanings can contradict the commonly understood intention. If you were learning a foreign language, you would expect to learn new ideas and new words. No one needs to tell you that you do not understand the foreign language. It is genuinely alien. With the General Theory of Action, however, you are led to "think" that you already understand the terms because you see familiar words and phrases. But the General Theory of Action is deceptively familiar. It does not appear alien, yet it is alien. The words you see like "action," "process," "actor," "personality," etc. all have a very unique set of meanings, and an important transforming context in the General Theory of Action -- Parsons' view of the nature of theory.

The General Theory of Action works on the fundamental assumption that there is a "real world." There are truly events going on, people doing things, and there are objects to be found and used. There is life, a world, and a universe surrounding us, and this has been so for a very long time. There **is** a real world.

There is a difference between the real world of

events and the words people use, however. Words are not the events they refer to. In fact, there are no words that can adequately display events in the real world. The scope of the real world is so vast, complex and constantly changing, that the General Theory of Action assumes that no words can adequately "say" the real world of events. As Max Weber put it, "life with its irrational reality and its store of possible meanings is inexhaustible. The <u>concrete</u> remains perpetually in flux, ever subject to change in the dimly seen future of human culture, an ever changing finite segment of the vast chaotic stream of events which flows away through time."[1] The real world then, is seen in the General Theory of Action as a living whole, infinite and unique in each moment, beyond any meager words or symbols which would be used to try and entrap it into some timeless conceptual form. No words can "say it all." Once any word is uttered or written the whole vast complex of living existence has changed again anyway.

Another assumption in the General Theory of Action is that words are human creations. What the human mind makes of the data that comes through the senses, and thinks about it, is always created. What we "see" is filtered through our senses, and comes into the consciousness mediated and incomplete. Words are critical in the ability of the mind to make sense out of what it "sees," but again, the words are not the events. They are only human creations used to manage the tremendous amount of sense data we encounter. Words are like the blind man's cane. He "sees" with his cane. Inside the human brain, there is no light, only an <u>idea</u> of light sparked by electrons racing from the senses to the neurons. We use the word "light" to symbolize the experience. Likewise, there is no such thing as gravity, or mass, or society. These too are words, artfully created by humanoids to manage complex experiences and communicate ways to manipulate what is encountered in the real world. Without the word, the experience in the consciousness would only be a mass of unrelated sense data. It is the word that creates a handle upon which to hang the experience. The order of the universe is not there for the mere looking. There is no way of pointing a finger or taking a picture of it. In a deep sense, order must be created. What we see, as we see it, is but disorder.

It is the creativeness of the scientist who comes up with new words that makes it possible to make connections, to map and join experiences. There is no such thing as "one" in the real world of events. No camel would encounter one, and no object "is" one and only one. We can look at a marble in a glass jar and think of one marble or one jar of marbles. The "one" is a concept created by us to refer to many objects and relate them to each other in varied ways. The object does not require being called "one." "Oneness" exists in the mind of the observer.

Theories are more complicated examples of this same human creativeness. The words of science are ideas about relationships, patterns and interconnections. This is also the case with the General Theory of Action. Parsons does not imply that there are such things as actors or Pattern Variables in the real world any more than a physicist supposes there is such a thing as mass or speed. The highly organized concepts of a theory make it possible to think about events and predict the consequences of sequences of behaviors. A theory is an idea-scheme -- though a very sophisticated scheme. It is not a picture of reality and its concepts are not intended to be taken as standing for realities. It is a map, and a map is not the road taken.

It is in this vein that Parsons calls theory a "Myth," or a "cognitive map."

> Society is not a TABULA RASA upon which things called "facts" inscribe their determinate and essential paths and shapes.... We approach our data as humans; and, as humans, we approach with differential receptivity and intentionality everything toward which we propose a cognitive

> orientation.... Data do not simply impose their structure on our inquiring and open minds: we **interact** with 'facts'. We are not naive, we are not innocent; and, as we shall argue, 'no fact is merely itself': a completely open mind is a completely empty one. There is a formative input to analysis, the components of which are not born EX NIHILO in or of the moment of encounter with 'facts'; rather, they are grounded in the orientation and frame of reference of the analyst. Indeed, in a major part we create, we do not merely encounter, facticity.[2]

Parsons goes on to say that "the facts of science are myths," and we select from what William James called 'booming, buzzing' reality; we establish boundaries, we ascribe limits.

> We exclude--and what we exclude haunts us at the walls we set up. We include--and what we include limps, wounded by amputation. And most importantly, we must live with all this. We must live with our wounded and our ghosts. There can be no Bultman of science, pleading that we 'de-mythologize.' ANALYTIC THOUGHT ITSELF IS MYTHOLOGIZATION.[3]

A. FACTS AND TRUTH

To further clarify Parsons' view, we need to define the word "fact." For Parsons, a "fact" is simply a <u>statement</u> that has been verified. The word "fact" refers to the <u>statement</u>, and does not refer to a phenomena or an event. In his words, "a fact is not a phenomena at all, but a <u>proposition about</u> one or more phenomena."[3] Thus, if someone says, "it is raining," we have someone's statement. They may look out the window or walk out the door, and verify, "yes, it is raining." The "fact" is still nothing more than the uttered or written statement that has been shown by observation to fit the events happening in the real world. In the General Theory of Action, when the term "fact" is used, it represents a human utterance, and is not the event in the real world.

If follows from this that "truth" means a series of connected statements called "facts" that have been verified. The truth is not a phenomena or an event. The focus is on the humanly created concepts and the way they fit with experiences in the real world. By using these creations, we find ourselves able to communicate with each other so we can organize life together so things get done, and have meaning. The other outcome of the invention of scientific language is the capacity to order the non-human elements of the world to build, travel, and otherwise effect our daily life.

B. REIFICATION

Scientific language is not without its problems. The most troublesome predicament is that it is easy to forget language is a medium of communication. Here the mind goes directly to the reference point of a word, disregarding the crucial part the word itself plays in the drama -- much as the fish forgets the water it swims about in every day. In "reification" people forget that words are human constructions. They forget words are simply sounds that people make and recognize. Instead, the word comes to imply hard reality. That works when we use words to warn, point, and otherwise identify objects we encounter in the real world. Not all words work that way however. Some words do not point to something a camel could encounter regardless of the word, like a rock. "Speed" is not a phenomena that exists somewhere anymore than "weight," "mass," "gravity," "role," or "society" does. These words do not designate "things" that exist. They are ideas people use to manage their reflections about the world.

Reification is especially troublesome in sociology. Here terms such as "society," "personality," "culture," "institution," etc. come to be thought of as realities with a force and power independent of people -- something which "eyes see and fingers grasp."[4] Eyes cannot see a family structure and fingers cannot grasp an economic system. A value, a tradition, a custom, a rule is not some "thing" that has a life of its own independent of words and the people who create them. Its life is in the breath of the conscious idea. What is a social system but an idea? Unearthing the temples of the Mayans does not tell what went on there, or why they were important. Somehow, there must be some firm trace of the ideas that defined the objects to make any sense of the ancient artifacts. When social scientists forget this fact, both they and their readers come to different conclusions about causes and effects than were perhaps originally intended.

In the General Theory of Action, it is especially important to recognize that Parsons sees the concepts of sociology as concepts, or human creations that do not have any reality in the real world in any other guise than that of an idea. He says that, "indeed, in major part we create, we do not merely encounter facticity."[5] The idea of a social system or a Pattern Variable functions much as numbers and processes do in mathematics. Since there is no "thing" which is undeniably "one," the number can be applied at will to any object or class of objects, depending on the perspective of the observer. Similarily, there is no such "thing" as a Pattern Variable, or a Social System that stands independent of ideas, and so people do not "have" Pattern Variables in their minds that social scientists "find." These concepts are but the instruments of the scientist whose aim is to develop empirical statements.

C. EMPIRICAL

For Parsons, "empirical" means that ideas can suggest behavior patterns that when actually carried out, will result in expected consequences in the real world.

The job of theory is to devise ways of thinking about the real world that make the prediction and manipulation of events possible. Theory is the instrument of prediction, not the elements of an event. For the physicist, it does not really matter if there is such a "thing" as "one," or "one atom of hydrogen," if the behaviors he directs result in a rocket engine firing. His device is theory -- a contrivance used to manage events to achieve a desired outcome. If his theory "works," it is true. It is the outcome that is tested. A theory is empirical if the propositions which can be drawn **from** theory, and **by means of** theory, are verified. The test is made upon the hypotheses generated from the whole theory. There are no articles in physics journals to prove or disprove the existence of "one," just as Parsons is not concerned about proving the existence of "Pattern Variables" or "Social Systems." The use of a ruler makes a good example of this point. The ruler is a device. It is **used** to measure, compare, and predict. The ruler is not what is measured, and the ruler cannot be used to measure itself, for it is that which measures. A different ruler can be used to measure the first ruler, but then it is a **different** ruler. It does not matter if the ruler is metric or based on the U.S. standard. There is no such "thing" as an "inch," and the usefulness of the ruler does not rely upon finding an "inch" existing in the real world. The ruler is not the objective sought, nor the conclusion to be drawn. It is the <u>device</u> used to "define" and "organize" data with a view to action. It all depends on the imagination of the person creating and using the ruler.

Thus, a theory is not thought of as a replica of reality in the General Theory of Action. Theory constitutes a sophisticated means of defining a situation, and consequently, an empirically verifiable theory or definition of the situation "consists in deliberately investigating phenomena with the expectations derived from theory in mind and seeing whether or not the facts actually found agree with these expectations."6 What follows, then, is not a theory of "action," but a THEORY of action.

3

THE BASIC ELEMENTS OF ACTION

Every theory starts with its own assumptions and vocabulary. As the theory is finally used, however, often these early assumptions drop into the background and are not used as integral parts of the working theory. This early exercise is seen as but a primary point of departure. This is true in the General Theory of Action and thus it is important to understand the fundamental assumptions about the Elements of Action and thier relationships to the mature theory.

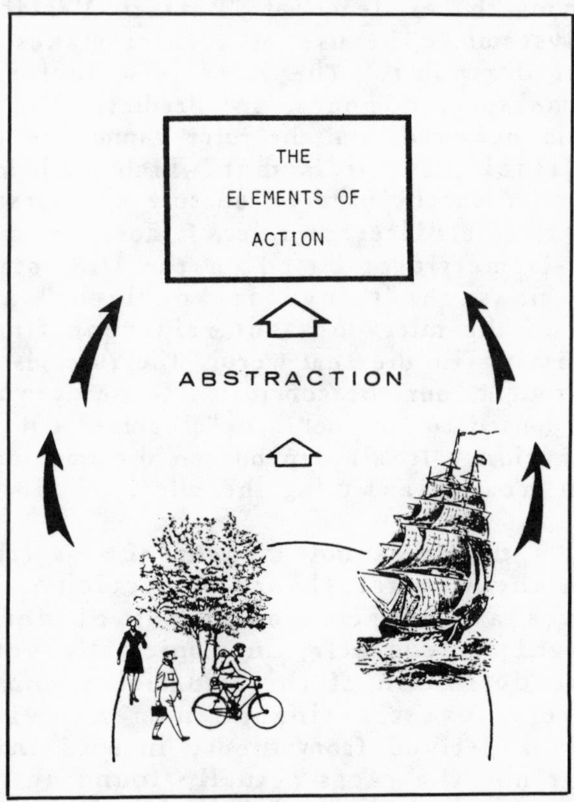

FIGURE 1

Figure 1 shows the Elements of Action as the prime departure point for the General Theory of Action. The assumptions included in the Elements of Action represent a supposition that sees the "real world" as fantastically complex, unique, and constantly in a process of change. Social life is thought of as a complexion of all the views of each individual person in an immediate situation, but who is also rooted to a past as well as the present through the medium of meanings and experiences while directing mind and actions toward others. People are the senders and receivers. Each person is real, and the ideas created about the world are as real as they are believed and thought to be.

Because this assumption sees the real world as so vastly complex and changing, many of the concepts in this part of the theory are rarely used in the theoretical analysis because of the nearly infinite variations that are possible. However, Parsons will neatly derive the aspects of the working theory from this first level of the Elements of Action.

Please turn to Plate II.

There are only three parts to the Elements of Action:

The Actor and Action

The Situation of Action

The Orientation of the Actor
to the Situation

If you look at the Diagram, you see the stick figure represents the Orientation of the Actor to the Situation and the "bottle" represents the Situation of Action.

I. THE ORIENTATION OF THE ACTOR TO THE SITUATION

A. THE ACTOR

Actors are <u>not</u> people; the concept does not refer to real, sweating persons. Actor is a theoretical concept that refers to a **system** of action. As far as the General Theory of Action is concerned, the term actor refers to a **system** or **pattern** and nothing more. As a **system** of action, the concept actor represents a system of systems of relationships. The concept actor is the unit of identification for the concepts included in the orientation to a situation.

Part of a circuit diagram to a television set is a good illustration of what the concept actor represents (see Figure 2). The circuit diagram is the "system of action" of the television unit. It is an actor. The diagram is not the set, and is not mistaken for the actual television. However, if something goes wrong, the diagram can be used to diagnose the problem and perform whatever operations are needed to get it fixed. The diagram does not look anything like the parts of the real set. This is also true of the relationship between a person and actor. "Actor" is to a real person as the theoretical circuit diagram is to a real television set. The author of the circuit diagram would not expect anyone to mistake the diagram for the real thing, and in fact, the circuit diagram represents no one specific set, but a type that applies to many sets. Likewise, the concept actor represents no one real person, and can be related to many people. There is much that applies to real people that is not even considered in the patterns included in the concept of actor.

Actor and the kinds of system designated by that word point to **systems** of relationships of motives and orientations to action. The emphasis is on the idea of **system**, and not on motives and orientations. Motives and orientations are part of the prepositional phrase "of..." which makes them descriptive, and not definitive.

They are important, but they are not the major idea. The significant factor is the emphasis on the idea of **systems.**

A CIRCUIT DIAGRAM

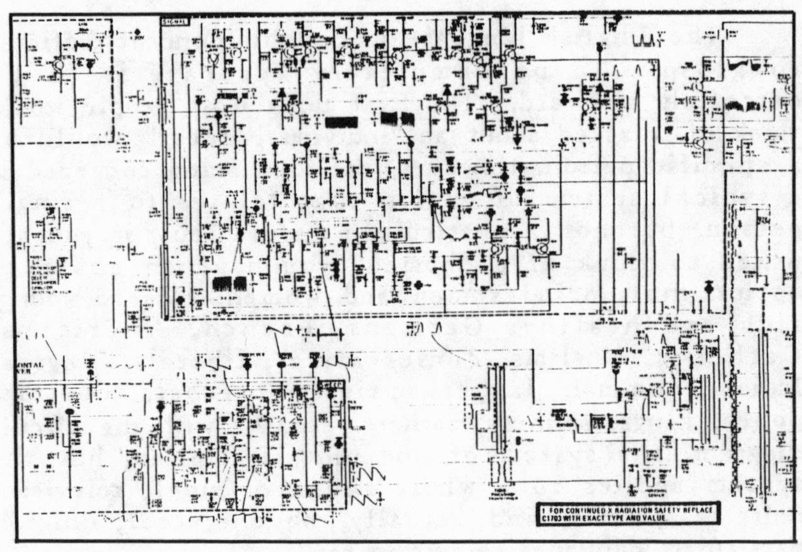

FIGURE 2

One example of the relationships implied in prepositional phrases can be seen in the statement that "the surfers of California love its beaches." The noun, or subject here is the surfers. The prepositional phrase is "of California." The surfers are not California. The prepositional phrase gives more information about the subject. In another example, "John is sick of beans." John is not beans, and sick is not beans; furthermore, not all beans are sick. John is the subject, and the major fact is that he is sick, in this case of beans.

"Beans" tells us the source of his sickness. It is more information about why and how. The same logic applies to the statement that an "actor is a system of action." The emphasis is on the system. The system is not the action anymore then the surfers are California or John is beans. "Of action" tells what **kind** of system is referred to.

1. Individual Actor

The English language makes this concept difficult to grasp. To be completely accurate is to be extremely awkward. The first thing most people would think of if asked about an "individual actor" would be a specific person. However, the idea being conveyed is a **typical** system of action that relates to a single person, but not a particular person. Thus, if you are asked to think of a "human" you have an abstract notion that includes men and women, old and young, sick and healthy, Germans, French, Americans, Catholics, Muslims, conservatives, liberals, Negros, Indians, criminals, lawyers, priests, teachers, doctors, popes, kings, mothers, fathers, etc. As with the circuit diagram, the system of one unit is implied, but the system applies to a whole range of single television units or systems, and actually, no one, real, unique, particular individual television set.

The concept of individual actor, then, refers to a **system** of organized motives and orientations arranged in a typical pattern, and indicating a single unit.

2. Actor as Collectivity

Since the definition of actor refers to a system of action, it follows that a collectivity is also an actor, since a collectivity is also **a system** of action.

Using the circuit system example again, it is possible to imagine a whole set of stereo components linked together into one system of sound. The interrelationships would be quite complex, yet each "individual" component would be a single unit or part of the larger system. What changes is the point of reference, or definition of what is "one." Each component could be considered a single system of action, and the whole sound system could be thought of as a single system of action.

There is nothing in the real world, then, which prescribes whether an action system is to be viewed as individual or as a collectivity. This distinction comes from the social scientist who makes the decision about the focus of the reference system. IBM can be thought of as an actor, or the President of IBM can be designated an actor. In both cases, the concern will be with **systems** of action.

B. ACTION

"Action" should not be thought of as some process "going on," but as a relationship. It refers to a relationship between systems or structures of systems. As such, "action" does not indicate behaving or doing.

From this perspective, addition and subtraction are "action" in so far as they are concerned with the relationships between number concepts. The relationship between a + b does not "do" anything. The plus sign does not "do" anything. The plus sign indicates a type of link between two systems, a and b. A minus sign would indicate another type of relationship, and hence a different kind of "action."

If you put two sticks at right angles, there is a right angle relationship. When the sticks are lying there on the ground, they are not "doing" anything. The "relationship" is not "acting," but it is a theoretical action in that there is proximity implied in the pattern of the sticks. In the same vein, a scientist can consider, mathematically, how close a space ship can come to a black hole before being sucked into it. The scientist does the figuring, and there is "action" in the theoretical relationship. All that appears on the paper is a series of numbers and formulas, and no one takes the dazzling ride.

Both of these examples show what Parsons means when he uses the term "action": the relationship between systems of action. Again, the English language makes this idea hard to keep in mind.

C. ACTOR AS A POINT OF REFERENCE

Please turn to Plate II for the discussion of parts C and D.

The actor system of action is the point of reference of the Theory of Action. It is through the perspective of the designated actor system of orientations that the Situation of Action itself is defined. The goals, objects, and boundaries to be included in a given situation are thus completely relative to the system of orientations or perspective of the designated actor system, called the "actor-ego" or "actor-subject" ("ego" is not used here in the Freudian sense, but as a direct derivation from the Latin word"ego", which stands for "I").

In the diagram on Plate II, the actor system of action is connected to a "bottle," defined as the Situation. According to the General Theory of Action, the Situation is only what is identified as a situation by some "actor" system of action. There is no real "situation," and this theoretical system is totally dependent on an actor system. Thus, if there are fifteen actor systems, the social scientist would need to think in terms of sixteen different situations -- those of the fifteen actor systems and the one for the social scientist.

Each Situation is composed of "elements." First is the goal or that state of affairs toward which the actor is oriented. Secondly are objects, which are defined by the actor system and are there because of the actor system (ship, tree, and man). Third are the normative limits or actor expectations of what should be done to achieve the goal, what should be done or done to objects, and which objects are "out of bounds" in the pursuit of the goal (flags, or the value of liberty, and money).

Since the Situation is relative to each actor system, there is no "situation as such" which can be thought to exist independent of the actor systems. Situations are relative to definition by the actor systems, thus there can be as many different situations are there as actor systems used. Furthermore, there is no reason that requires the situations to coincide. Situation is purely a matter of perspective.

Figure 3 is an example of this point. The social scientist has designated two actor systems for analysis. (This has nothing to do with how many could be designated, as it is purely the prerogative of the scientist). Each actor system, A and B, has a "Definition of the Situation" related to its perspective. The Definition of the Situation of Actor A includes some of the same things as those included by B (money, woman and tree), and both A and B include things not included by the other (A: The value of Justice, money, man and girl; B: flag, baby carriage, man on a bicycle, and the value of freedom). The social scientist is completely dependent on these perspectives, and is not to include any additional material as part of the situation, regardless of how important it may be considered.

A representative illustration can be used about a hit record. A chemical analysis of the record would be totally limited to the material contained in the record, and the chemicals used in the manufacture process, etc. On the other hand, an artistic analysis would be concerned with colors, design, graphics, etc. In this case, even though the object in the situation, the record, would be the same for both actor system A (chemical perspective) and actor system B (artistic perspective) what would be seen and considered important would be totally different. Furthermore, the musical quality or the popularity of the record would be irrelevant to each of these perspectives, no matter how important that might be to the social scientist doing the study.

One important implication of this theoretical assumption made by Parsons is that the sociologist cannot "play God" so to speak, and assume his own view of a situation is what counts as the major standard of evaluation. Rather, all situations are "relative" to the system of action through which they are viewed. The sociologist, to make any headway in the understanding of social phenomena, must see theory as a device that helps separate the theorist from his own point of view as much as possible. This will make it possible to recognize the many alternative ways a given situation can be viewed.

TWO VIEWS OF A SITUATION

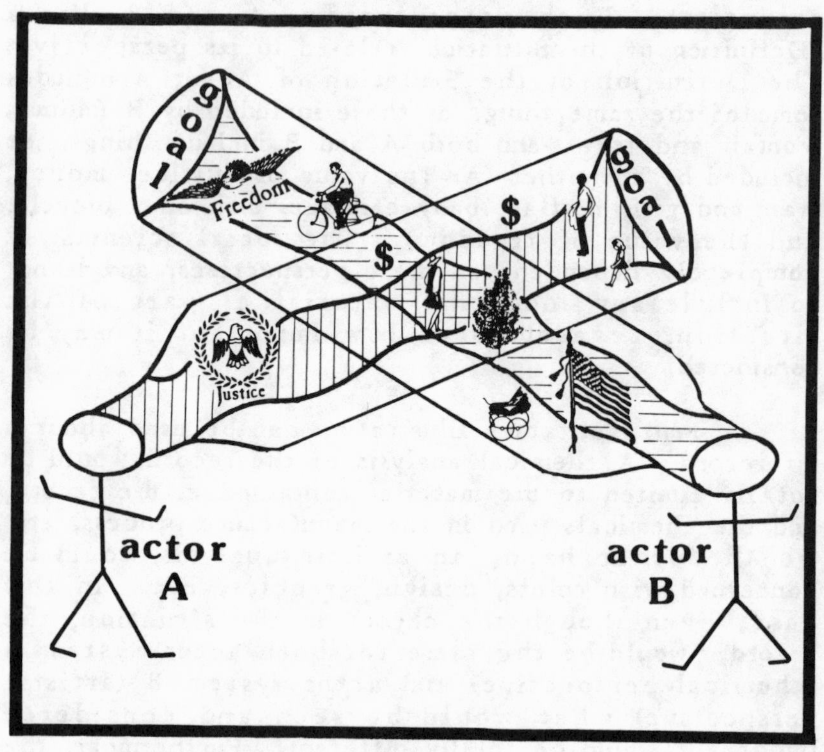

FIGURE 3

1. Objects

There are a number of different types of objects included in Plate II. The General Theory of Action defines two kinds of objects:

a. social
b. non-social
i. cultural
ii. physical

Any object, regardless of the type, is only "in a situation" if it is there from the point of view of the actor system as a subject. The "presence" or "absence" of objects, then, is completely relative.

Not only is the presence of an object a function of the perspective of the actor-ego, so is its type. An object "is" whatever the actor-ego defines it to be.

a. Social Objects: A social object is one which the actor-ego **thinks** is a social object. That is, the actor-ego expects the object to be socially responsive and defines the object as having a system of orientations, motive systems, etc. Since the object is only social if the actor defines it as social, it follows that another actor-ego could define the same object as non-social. Thus, a "purse" can be defined as a social object. If an actor-ego defines a "purse" as "mother," and "talks" to it, and waits to hear for an answer which is fully expected to come, then the "purse" is considered by the social scientist as a social object.

In a situation, if an actor-ego defines an object as a social object, it is usually referred to in the General Theory of Action as an "actor-alter." In this case the term "alter" comes again from the Latin, meaning "other." Hence, actor-ego, refers to the actor system designated as a subject, and the actor-alter as another social object in the situation as defined by the actor-ego. To trim down the verbage, this is often referred to as simply "actor" or "ego" and "alter."

b. Non-social Objects: Objects which the

actor-ego defines as not being social, as not having attitude systems, as not possessing systems of orientation, and hence not capable of "interacting" or responding to the actor-ego are called "non-social objects." Examples are cars, rocks, chemicals, rivers, clouds, etc.

From the point of view of the actor-ego, some objects that one actor sytem might define as a social object, such as patients in a hospital, might be defined as a non-social objects by another actor system. This was the point in the television series, "My Mother the Car" where one of the characters thought her mother had been reincarnated in an old car, and part of the fun was the response that came when others, who defined the car as a non-social object, found it doing inconsistent things. In both the book and movie rendition of ONE FLEW OVER THE CUCKOO'S NEST there is another example of this situation. The story takes place in a mental institution where some patients are able to walk around, and some are so incapacitated they are strapped up to the wall for the day. Most of the patients and the orderlies define those strapped up to the wall as "vegetables" and thus define them as non-social objects with no feelings, orientations, motives, or ability to respond. The hero, McMurphy, however, defines them as social objects, and even is able to get some minimal response from them. This was also the point in the movie "The Elephant Man" where some saw the man disfigured by disease as a social object, and many others saw him as a commodity, a freak, a display -- a non-soical object.

<u>i. Culture Objects:</u> Cultural objects are defined by an actor-ego as non-social elements of tradition, heritage, laws, ideas, etc. which become the focus of the orientation of some actor-ego. The actor-ego "pays attention" to some law or value, making it a focal point for concentration. Thus a group of law students could be having a debate about some criminal or civil law.

Cultural objects can be transmitted from one

actor-system to another, and internalized with no "loss" in the transmission process. A teacher who passes the ideas of mathematical processes to a student does not "lose" them in the process. In the beginning, the teacher knows them, and at the end, the teacher still knows them as well as some of the students to whom they have been passed. One can "take" an idea, but no one can "take away" an idea so that it is "gone."

ii. Physical Objects: Physical objects are those objects defined as non-social objects which are considered as a material, solid entities that can be manipulated and possessed, such as a ship.

A fundamental point here, and one that pervades the whole General Theory of Action is that objects are "in" a situation only from the perspective of some theoretical actor-ego system. Situations do not exist independent of an actor-system's definition of them. The assumption that this represents about the real world is that situations do not exist independent of some human definition of them as a situation. Situation is a human idea since a "state of affairs" is the human mantle placed upon the real world by humans to give it meaning and significance.

c. Modalities of Objects

Modalities are defined a properties of an object, or "aspects" of an object which are significant to an actor-ego. The number and type of modalities is found by looking through the perspective of the actor-ego. It follows that anything that has meaning for an actor-ego is a modality, and modalities are relative. There is no absolute number or type of modality. No object has some "real," given number of modalities which are "there" present in the object, to be "discovered" by observation of the object. The "medium" of the actor-ego is always necessary to determine modality, and modalities may vary with different actor-egos. From the point of view of one actor-ego system, an object can be "beautiful," to another "ugly," and to another simply "useful" -- a true case of the point that "beauty is in the eye of the beholder." A modality, then, is any aspect of an object deemed significant by an actor-ego system.

An object can be defined as a goal, resource, means, condition, obstacle, symbol or norm.

2. Goals

Goals are objects which happen to be some "end to be attained" in a situation or state of affairs which is anticipated and defined by an actor-ego system. As objects, goals are relative to the actor-ego's systems of orientation. A goal, then, can be anything the actor-ego defines as an object in a situation and which becomes the end to be attained or achieved.

3. Normative Limits

In the orientation of an actor-ego to a goal and to objects in a situation, there are also a set of "norms," or what the actor-ego considers as the "rules" or expected ways of action to be followed, along with the perceived sanctions of reward or punishment for following or violating these perceived "norms."

In attaining the goal of "getting a new car," for example, the actor-ego has the norm that "stealing" the object, car, is "wrong." In paying for a traffic ticket, the actor-ego may have a norm that "showing respect" for the judge is "right" and "being late" or "talking back" is "wrong," i.e., against the perceived rules. Norms are thus expectations about what to do or not do, and how it should or should not be done. They are rules and standards for behavior.

The normative limits, like all other aspects of the situation, are only relevant or included from the perspective of the actor-ego. If the actor-ego defines certain norms as meaningful in a given situation, no matter what _type_ of meaning is used, or who agrees with that meaning, those norms constitute the "normative limits" of the situation. Norms not recognized by the actor-ego are not considered part of the situation.

On the East coast, for example, there are many rules on the law books called "Blue Laws." They date back many years, and for the most part are neither known nor followed. There is one law that sets a fine for not tearing across the tax stamp placed on the top of every pack of cigarettes sold. Most people just tear open the top third of the package for easy access. Neither the people nor the police know of the rule, and thus do not even think about it. A law has to be thought of to be enforced.

D. THE SITUATION

This term refers to whatever the actor-ego "includes" in the system of orientations in relation to some given goal. Situation, then, is the one concept which summarizes all the elements of action discussed so far. It includes actor, object, goals, and norms, the way they are defined by an actor-ego, and the way they are related to each other by an actor-ego system. It "means," actor, objects, goals and norms. There are as many potential situations as there are potential actor-egos which can be stipulated by the social scientist.

The focus of the situation, then, is not on people, but on **SYSTEMS** of action and orientations that are typical of people, but not replicas of people. The concepts are devices designed and created to establish theoretical assumptions related to the real world. There is no such thing as an "actor" alive and walking around in the real world. The concepts used in defining a situation are similar to those used in the electronic circuit diagram. They are a system or pattern of relationships that designates "types" that fit the real world, but they are not what they represent.

II. THE ORIENTATION OF THE ACTOR

One of the defining categories used for a social actor-system is "orientation." The orientation of the actor-ego is the mechanism used to determine the situation. (See Plate I). It is the focus of the orientation of the actor-ego that identifies objects, goals, and normative limits. An elaboration of the elements of the Orientation of the Actor can be found in Plate III which is to be used for all of section II.

The Orientation of the Actor is seen as a "conception" which is, "explicit, implicit, conscious or unconscious." It includes systems of what the actor "wants," systems of what is "seen" or how things "look," and systems of "plans of action."

The "conception" of the situation at the front of the diagram is broken down into three theoretically separated processes: cognition, cathexis, and evaluation (in large capital letters). Each of these three processes has two aspects, the Cultural level (in script) and the Need Disposition level (in modern slanted script).

A. COGNITION, CATHEXIS, AND EVALUATION

1. Cognition

Cognition deals with the aspect of "recognizing" or "seeing" an object. In cognition, the actor "locates" an object, sees what it "is," what it "is not," what it is "used for," and what it "does." The actor "fits" the object together with other objects. This seeing is described as "cognitive mapping." So, when a given actor sees an object with a propeller, large wings, motors, etc., he recognizes an "airplane." Some other actor from another culture might "recognize" a "bird-god." Or, when an actor confronts a little piece of plastic attached to a wall, he "recognizes" a light switch. Having small children around can highlight the significance of cognition tremendously. What an adult actor sees as "chair," the child actor may see as "castle" or "tank." What the adult actor sees as a fragile vase, the child sees as something which "bursts apart into a million pieces" when dropped. What the adult actor sees as "fire that can hurt and burn" the child actor sees as "pretty to touch." In cognition, then, an actor system identifies objects in an environment and fits them to concepts present in the system.

2. Cathexis

Cathexis is the investment of an object with "want" or "not want" meaning. This level relates to how the actor "feels" about the object in terms of being hurt by it, or getting satisfaction or pleasure out of it. A Frenchman may see snails cooking and "want" some. An American tourist on the other hand, may "not want" them, and in fact may become nauseous at the thought of eating snails. Cathexis refers to the perception ot the desirability or potential gratification or lack of gratification of an object.

3. Evaluation

Evaluation refers to "what the actor plans to do" about what is seen, wanted or not wanted. The process of evaluation specifically means the "organization" of the cognitive and cathectic modes into a "choice." This concept will be more completely discussed after other elements of the Orientation of the Actor are covered.

B. INTERNALIZED CULTURE STANDARDS
(script letters and slanted lines)

Culture Standards refer to rules or systems of meanings according to which selection or choices are to be made. They represent sets of "pre-made" decisions, definitions, and standards which have been selectively "internalized" by an actor-system from the Culture System (both of these terms will be defined in later chapters).

1. Cognitive Standards of Relevance

Cognitive Standards of Relevance means that the actor-system has a set of rules and definitions for determining what things "are" and what uses they can have. Language is an important aspect of these standards. "Chair" is a word which not only identifies a set of objects, it also designates the expected use for the object -- a place to sit. Words and their accompanying meaning act as a set of guides for identifying objects in a situation. If a customer walks into a furniture store and sees a huge "bean bag" in a corner, he may be confused about what the object is, and what purpose it has. When he hears it is a "chair" the problem is solved.

Cognitive Standards also involve rules for what is to be seen as "important" or as "valid." Seeing a group of children yelling and shouting is not necessarily important. They are probably "playing." Seeing a group of children yelling and shouting and running from dog frothing from the mouth is important. There is "danger" from the dog. The Cultural Standards, then, define the limits of "play" and "danger," the qualities of a "serious problem" and "letting off steam," etc.

When confronting any "situation," then, the actor-system has available a whole system of Cultural Standards of Relevance to use in deciding what an object "is," and deciding what kind of object it is -- what it will do, etc. In some instances, if the culture does not have a word or a set of rules for defining an object, it may not be "seen" by the actor at all. Twigs arranged in a special way tell the Indian that a bear is near, but a modern city person might not even notice the twigs, let alone the arrangement. In a sense, the actor-system "encounters" a situation by means of these standards of relevance, and in the absence of a standard, encounters nothing.

2. Cathectic Standards of Appropriateness

Standards of Cathexis, or "wants," on the Cultural

Level become Standards for Appreciation. This category <u>excludes</u> anything to do with "goodness" or "badness," "rightness" or "wrongness." Appreciation refers to "liking" something, "enjoying" it, having a sense of proper "fit," or the opposite -- "disliking," "not enjoying," or "out of fit." The actor-system has a whole set of such cultural rules to be used to decide what is appropriate. These standards, like the Cognitive Standards, are internalized aspects of the Cultural System of which the actor-system is a member. The culture provides the actor with a ready-made program of criteria for what should be enjoyed, what is appropriate, what is to be appreciated, and all the accompanying opposites.

Music is a good illustration of this point. People from Western cultures, Europe, the United States, etc., often do not like the classical music from the Oriental cultures. They find it displeasing and the tones disconcerting. In some other examples, it is considered inappropriate to scotch tape pictures to living room wallpaper made of India silk. It is considered inappropriate to go to a fancy ball in a formal dress and tennis shoes, or pick your nose while dancing. Not bathing for a week before the dance is also not considered appropriate.

There is no moral regulation involved in what is liked or not liked. There is nothing morally wrong with not bathing, wearing tennis shoes to fancy balls, etc., but many would find it terribly inappropriate, and not "like" it, or like to do it. What is "likeable" then is relative to the rules or Standards of Appropriateness of a given culture.

<u>3. Moral-Evaluative Standards</u>

Cultural Standards of Evaluation are defined as standards of responsibility or moral standards. Here consequences must be taken into account, and responsibility is given to the actor-system in terms of the results of choices. In the evaluative mode, the actor-system "considers" the consequences and attached responsibility according to these cultural standards. The decision or choice that is made then, is weighed according to these cultural definitions of moral categories--rules for right and wrong.

There are two categories of these moral standards. The first includes consequences to the integration of the personality system of the actor-system: there are things an actor-system must not do to itself. The second covers the consequences to the integration of social systems the actor-system participates in as a member: there are things an actor-system must not do to others.

This means that there are cultural and social rules for what an actor-system can and cannot do, defined as right and wrong. Some of the effects of some actions are not acceptable, and the actor-system must be prepared to take the responsibility for those actions.

In the first case suicide or self-destruction with the use of drugs is considered immoral and illegal. In the second case, if an actor "kills," the effect is deemed "wrong" and the actor has to realize there are culturally and socially defined penalities. These are moral criteria for choice, or the cultural rules for what is "right" and "wrong" that an actor uses to "evaluate" what should and should not be done.

The clue to the internalized cultural ethic is guilt. If the actor has "internalized" a set of moral imperatives, there will be "guilt" or "shame" associated with violations of the code. If the actor has the ethic that it is wrong to cheat, then a transgression would be accompanied by reactions of guilt such as sweating, nervousness, anxiety, blushing, etc.

There are, then, three sets of cultural standards "internalized" into an actor-system: Standards of Cognition, Standards of Cathexis, and Standards of Evaluation.

C. THE SYSTEM OF NEED DISPOSITIONS
(slanted print and straight dotted lines on diagram)

Need Dispositions are basic tendencies or fundamental inclinations toward some type of completion or fulfillment. They have a deep-seated imperative which can vary in intensity from weak to overpowering. Connected to the physiological or viserogenic aspects of the actor, they are more than simply detached "ideas" to be used or not. They have a pervasiveness throughout the actor system that can "make him sweat," and at times can overpower consciously held Standards of Evaluation. They are a forceful aspect of the Personality System.

1. Cognition

The Need Dispositions are an important factor in the systems of Cognition in the actor. For instance, if an actor had been on a strict juice diet for three weeks, and a steak dinner was placed on a table along with a $1,000 bill, the probability is that the actor would only "see" the steak dinner. The money, at that point, would not be relevant, and hence might not be "recognized" at all. Quizzed later, such an actor might not even remember the money was on the table. In another case, an actor with little money tends to pay a lot of attention to prices, while one extremely affluent may be totally oblivious to the costs of things. The point is that the System of Need Dispositions can influence what is "seen" in a situation to a significant degree.

2. Cathexis

Need dispositons have an equivalent effect on Cathexis, or what is wanted. The hungry actor "wants" food. Even a pet puppy dog might appear as a sweet morsel if an actor had a strong enough need disposition to eat. It might even happen that this actor could "like" the idea of eating the puppy in such a circumstance. It would be quite "fitting" given the perspective of the situation. The need then, could be so strong that what is "wanted" in the situation is a significant reflection of the need disposition.

Similarly, the actor who "needs" love, is "happy" when it is given. That actor experiences "joy at being praised," "gloom" at not being noticed, "pain" at being overlooked or criticized. This actor "needs" attention, and hence "likes" it when it comes.

The needs of an actor-system, then, can affect what is "wanted"or "liked," even in opposition to the Cultural Standards, though that is usually not the case. The actor who "needs" attention may "like" the results of getting in trouble, dressing in an atrocious fashion, and pasting magazine pictures on the wall if it brings the much needed attention. The Need Dispositions of the actor, then, can effect what the actor "likes," "wants," what gives "gratification," what is "satisfying," and what is "pleasing" or "repulsive."

3. <u>Evaluation</u>

Choice is made at this level in accordance with the kind of balance which results between the internalized Cultural Standards and the Need Dispositions of a typical actor-system.

D. CHOICE

It is at the level of evaluation that there is an integration of the cognitive, cathectic, and evaluative aspects of conception (regardless of the degree of importance given to Culture Standards and Need Dispositions). It is at this point that there is a "connection" to the available bodily energy of the actor-system. As all the perceptions come together into a "conception of the situation," there is a triggering, or mobilization of energy so the body can carry out intended action to "fit" the decision -- an orientation of the actor to the situation. If the bodily energy is <u>not</u> mobilized, a "choice" was never made to carry out such action.

For example, students often promise themselves they are going to do some hard studying during the evening. The books are there, but the eyes sag, the head droops, and they finally decide they are too tired to study, and get ready to go to bed. But friends call saying there is a surprise party. All of a sudden there is a burst of energy. The actor "wakes up," all ready to go! Analyzing this situation shows there never was a "choice" to study because the bodily energy was never mobilized in that direction. However, the actor <u>did</u> choose to go to the party, for energy was "turned on" when the opportunity came. For a choice, an actor must "tell the body to move" in order to fully carry out the orientation.

In the event the action is not carried out, the General Theory of Action holds that if energy was mobilized, that particular orientation of the actor should be accepted. So, if the party-going student fell and broke a leg, ending up at the local hospital instead of the party, the orientation of action was still directed toward the party -- a choice was made.

In summary, Plate III shows the conception of the situation as conscious, unconscious, explicit, or implicit. There are three elements which are considered to be aspects of the situation:

a) Cognition
b) Cathexis
c) Evaluation

Each element, cognition, cathexis, and evaluation has two aspects to it:

a) Standards of Internalized Culture
b) Drives stemming from Need Dispositions

Both are constantly involved in the cognition, cathexis and evaluation, but the degrees and significance can vary so that at one time Cultural Standards may be the most influential in determining the cognition, cathexis, and evaluation, while at another time the Need

Dispositions may predominate. Most of the time Cultural Standards and Need Dispositions are in harmony, but on occasion they may be in conflict. Finally, Choice is the completion of the orientation of a typical actor-system to a situation where bodily energy is mobilized and selectively directed by means of the conception of the situation.

The integration of Plate II and Plate III, The Definition of the Situation and the Orientation of the Actor to the Situation (which is actually an elaboration of the Actor system in the Definition of the Situation) completes the Elements of Action.

Parsons does not use this level in his working theory as it is too complex and would be very difficult. Imagine (or even try) listing **all** the elements of a situation from the point of view of even two or three actors over a fifteen or twenty minute conversation. Is your written list complete? Does it stand true to the tone and meaning of words, the intensity of the exchange, or even the levels of emotions felt? Can you even identify these factors accurately? Parsons abstracted from this level to Systems of Action instead. He uses the Elements of Action as the assumptions or theoretical base for the primary General Theory of Action.

II. ACTION AGAIN

This brings us full circle in the explanation of the Orientation of the Actor to the Situation, and hence in the portrayal of the Elements of Action. Action is the theoretical relationship between the structural system of the actor-ego and the structural system of the situation. The focus is upon "relationships" in the theoretical realm of relationships between systems. "Acting" is **NOT** what is meant. Real sweaty persons doing real acting in the real world is **NOT** what the Theory of Action is directly concerned with in its studies. The focus is upon **typical** patterns, systems, and relationships. The theory is thus "empirical" because these systems are used to develop hypotheses and plans for experimental behaviors in the real world to see if they work. Remember, the concepts in the General Theory of Action are not to be thought of as mirrors of the real world, but rather devices used to design explanations for behavior as well as systems of behaviors. This is especially true for the Elements of Action -- the springboard to the General Theory of Action.

4

THE THREE SYSTEMS OF ACTION

The Elements of Action are not generally used in the General Theory of Action simply because they are too complex. Each concept reflects the vast uniqueness and intricacy of not only one situation, but of all the potential actors who could be designated as a point of reference for situations. Furthermore, any actor-system can be thought of as a vast potential of orientations to an infinite number of potential situations. The point made by the discussion of these Elements of Action is that the real world, when viewed theoretically, is an infinite and complicated matter which is far beyond the grasp of humanly created concepts. Clarification of the Elements of Action is a starting point for the construction of the first actual level of the General Theory of Action.

Plate I shows the relationship of the "real world" to the Elements of Action outlined in Chapter II. The next level shown is the abstraction of three systems of action from the fundamental Elements of Action: Culture System, Social System, and Personality System.

These three systems are three views or qualities abstracted from the Elements of Action, and thus are not considered "elements" that should be thought of as separate from each other. They are three features or qualities of the same thing, the Situation of Action.

Culture Systems refer to systems of meanings.

Social Systems refer to systems of ways of behaving.

Personality Systems refer to systems of motivation.

I. THE CULTURE SYSTEM

Culture System refers to patterns of disembodied meanings, i.e., meanings abstracted from the Situation of Action. "Meaning" indicates systems of values, beliefs, symbols, etc. It signifies the "sense" of ideas, the patterns of priorities, the core of thoughts. In this sense, the term "culture" differs from what is found in most sociology text books, for there, the term also includes norms and motives, or everything that is learned. The General Theory of Action sharpens the distinctions made by this term and only refers to the meaning aspects of action, as distinguished from the patterns of behavior and motivations. This view is taken because a pattern of behavior can have different, if not conflicting patterns of meanings associated with it. For example, "hitting" someone hard on the upper arm would usually indicate hostility. However, in some blue collar systems, it can also mean friendship and inclusion in a group. The behavior system is the same for both groups but the meaning systems are contrary. In a system like the General Theory of Action, it is important to illuminate such dissimilarities, and hence a narrow definition of Culture System is used. Furthermore, the definition in the General Theory of Action is not directly concerned with the real meanings people use in everyday life, but rather with systems of typical meanings and the patterns of relationships between meaning systems.

As such, Culture System refers to a system of constellations of meanings, values, beliefs and symbols. It refers to the "meaning part" of an actor-system, the "meaning part" of objects, goals, alters, roles, etc. Every pattern of action, then, has its "meaning aspect."

To look at disco bands from the perspective of Culture System, the focus would be on the "meaning" of lyrics, the "meaning" of clothing, names of instruments, and the value or significance of the music. The tones used, the ways of moving to the sounds, the decibel levels would not be considered, unless their "meaning aspect" is the subject of attention. Of course, it would be impossible to "really" separate the meanings from the types of sounds and movements in the "real world." That is why such systems emphasize angles, for there are no "parts" that correspond to Culture System, Social System, or Personality System much as there is no top or bottom to a piece of bread. It is all in your viewpoint.

A. FOUR PHASES OF THE CULTURE SYSTEM

Parsons divides each of these systems into four aspects. Outlined here, the complete significance of this division will not become completely clear until later on as the theory is developed.

In the General Theory of Action there are four types of meaning systems, and these are generally depicted in the following format:

COGNITIVE SYMBOLIZATION	EXPRESSIVE SYMBOLIZATION
EXISTENTIAL INTERPRETATION	MORAL-EVALUATIVE CATEGORIZATION

FIGURE 4

At first glance, there should be two familiar categories: Cognitive and Moral-Evaluative.

1. Cognitive Symbolization

This aspect of Culture System is related to the identification of "what is," etc. It is the set of standards implied in cognition in the Orientation of the Actor to the Situation. However, it lacks "internalized" status on the level of the Culture System. In the Culture System, it is the **organized set of symbols and meanings which are related to the recognition, identification, and specification of objects or situations.** It is this set of symbols which designates "dog," "car," "pencil," "play," "work," "love," "riot," and "party." Cognitive symbols, then, tell us what things are. The Eskimo shaman knows what a fetish means, the Samurai knows what white means, and the American knows what the words, sounds, and gestures related to the Fourth of July mean, etc. When knowledge of these cognitive symbols is inadequate, misunderstandings can result with all sorts of consequences.

2. Expressive Symbolization

This concept is an abstraction from the internalized "Cathectic Standards" of the Orientation of the Actor to the Situation. It refers to the symbolism and meaning of appropriateness or wanting and not wanting. As such, it includes not only the standards of meaning themselves, but also the meaning of "punishments" or "rewards" that go along with those standards. Thus, dressing in a bathing suit is not suitable for a job interview for an executive position with a large bank, and such a behavior would carry a "meaning." To the interviewer, the situation may symbolize deviance or disrespect. To the person in the bathing suit, it may represent freedom or independence. At the Academy Awards in Hollywood each year, the men are expected to dress appropriately, in formal wear with a tux, white tie, etc. When one of the winners comes to receive the award without his tie, and sporting a white scarf, it is a violation of the standards of appropriateness, and within the Hollywood community that is symbolic of independence and a bit of creativity. "Liking" certain kinds of food, art, or music is also symbolic, and carries with it a meaning. People who like extremely modern music which has no melody, and which to many others violates their standards of appropriateness for music, may represent the creative artistry of the day, or symbolize a small elite in the musical community. Expressive Symbolization represents the meaning aspect of what is considered appropriate, wanted or not wanted, liked or not liked in a given Culture System.

3. Moral-Evaluative Categorization

This category pertains to systems of meanings for right or wrong, good or bad. These cultural values include the whole basis for moral behavior and attendant punishments or rewards. It is the meaning of "must not" or "it is a sin to." The Ten Commandments outline the meaning of a whole range of behaviors as does the Koran, etc. As with other aspects of the Culture System, the pattern of behavior is not the area of concern, but rather the **system of meaning of a behavior**, which is different. One illustration may clarify this system. Three people live in a house, the parents and a teenager. The parents leave $100 in a drawer in the living room in case anyone in the family runs into a temporary problem and needs money. If any of the people in the house take the money, it does not mean they "stole" it. However, if a friend of the family is staying in the house and "takes" the money, the meaning of that act might be designated "stealing" since the money did not belong to the houseguest and no permission was given to use it. If a stranger breaks into the house and takes the money, the meaning of the action is clearly "stealing." In some cases, if the teenager takes the money it might be defined as "stealing," though rarely would this be the case if either of the parents took the money. The behavior involved in opening the drawer and lifting out the money is the same for any of the people involved, but the meaning changes, and hence the moral implications for the action. Again, this category of Moral-Evaluative Categorization is an abstraction from the Moral-Evaluative Standards of the Actor in the Situation of Action.

4. Existential Interpretation

Existential Interpretation refers to the "ground of meaning" or the "basic premises" that justify and legitimize all the other systems of meaning of a Culture System. As the most fundamental phase of the Culture System, it provides the means of "making sense" of all the other values, beliefs, and symbols on the other three levels. Whenever a question is raised about a value on some other level, its explanation or support is found on the Existential Interpretation level. For example, in many culture systems, "life" is primary. The preservation of life in all its forms is very important. Killing animals for food is "explained" as preserving human life. Pollution control is part of the respect and care for all life on the planet. The value of respect for life is the "ground of meaning" and basis of legitimacy for other beliefs and symbols related to life. It is the "why" behind medical research and practice, laws about qualities of food and cleanliness, jogging and exercise, non-smoking and alcoholic clinics, and even moving mankind off the planet to live in space. In another society the "ground of meaning" may be in the "community." The "community" is more important than the life of its members, and so they can be sacrificed with justification for the good of all. Members marry whomever they are assigned to marry, take any job assigned, turn their children over for training at an early age, etc. In some cases the individual may "destroy himself" for the welfare of the community. Rewards are only given to those actions or situations which reinforce the community and punishment comes to those who put their own life or comfort before that of the group. The "value behind all values," the "essential meaning", the fundamental belief, in this type of society then is "the preeminence of the community." It is basic to the whole texture of thought and belief in that society.

The concept of Existential Interpretation, then, refers to the system of meaning behind meanings, the value behind values, the belief behind beliefs. It is at this level that the basic assumptions and foundations of the Culture System are represented.

II. THE PERSONALITY SYSTEM

Personality System refers to neither persons, nor to "personality" in the sense of having "charm," "charisma" or personal distinction. Rather it is concerned with **systems** of orientation and motivation about what is thought and felt and seen.

At first the Personality System may appear to be quite similar to the Culture System. However the Personality System refers to the translation of meanings, values, and beliefs into systems of orientation and motivation. This happens by means of incorporation into the system of need dispositions. Knowing values is not the same as being moved to act by them.

Orientation is the mobilization of bodily energy toward action, and corresponds to the typical ways in which meanings are connected to the physical-emotional matrix which triggers and sustains behavior. Without such a system of integration of ideas into the physical-emotional levels, no action at all would be possible and the Personality System would have no coherence, no identity, no means of actualizing self, making choices or directing behavior. Chaos would be the result -- total disintegration and loss of identity. A Personality System is a <u>system</u> of orientations towards actions which are rooted in the physical-emotional matrix of need-dispositions.

A. INTERNALIZATION

To understand the concept of the Personality System it is necessary to look into the idea of Internalization and its implications in the General Theory of Action.

Need dispositions can be thought of as **basic tendencies** or **fundamental inclinations** that tend toward fulfillment. They represent a deep-seated imperative which is connected to the physiological or viserogenic aspects of an actor. Need dispositions are more than simply detached "ideas" to be followed or not. They have a pervasiveness throughout the typical actor that can not only "make him sweat" but at times can overpower his consciously held standards of evaluation. They are a forceful aspect of the

Personality System.

From the point of view of the General Theory of Action, babies are born with a "generalized tendency toward well-being." They have a need disposition to experience "well-being" regardless of how it is produced or by whom it is rendered. At birth this need is amorphous, unformed, and undefined. There are no specifics, no pre-ordained ways for achieving well-being. It is a deep, imperative, yet nebulous drive.

In various actions, this tendency toward well-being is actualized, and it is through this "process" that the need develops its form and character. The situation in which the need for well-being is met comes to be associated with the need. In fact, there develops a need for the specific elements of the situation that have been experienced with well-being, and through a gradual process of historical growth, the need becomes allied with the ways or circumstances for themselves. These "ways" of meeting the need for well-being come to be needed, and it is the realization of some of the "ways" or aspects of the situation which then produce a feeling of well-being. In a given biography, the need can come to be attached to situations, action systems, or circumstances quite remote from the ones originally offered to the baby. Moreover, babies in unlike situations can experience well-being quite differently which explains some of the variations found from culture to culture.

For example, some people associate well-being with being peacefully alone while others are happiest surrounded with many people. Some people delight in confronting a difficult problem and trying to solve it alone, while others feel better when helped by someone else. These needs can go so far as to be associated with advertised products like cigarettes or soft-drinks through a complex process of replacement. A person whose well-being is actualized by being alone may be drawn to ads showing people alone in all kinds of natural environments, while others are attracted to ads showing lots of people, etc. Buying the cigarettes or soft-drink is rather like buying some phase of expected well-being and that can become a need in itself. In another case, hearing a specific song may bring a sense of well-being because the song is associated with good times, as with Christmas carols. In fact, changes in some carols, or even in some of customs associated with traditional holidays may be very upsetting to some people. Not meeting the need for well-being can have the effect of generating stress and strain.

No one is born with specific needs. Rather they are viewed as a typical biographical-historical development stemming from the ways the early "general tendency toward well-being" was satisfied, arching through a complex passage to the present system of need dispositions.

Internalization is more than learning the situations in which well-being is experienced. It also includes the intertwining of ideas with physical states of pleasure and pain. Learning to excell can be associated with intense physical gratification, and cheating can be accompanied by intense anxiety and bodily stress. Internalized value standards are therefore intimately connected with need dispositions in various degrees. Personality System deals with the typical values articulated in systems of drives and the energy mobilized by the body into behavior through choice by a typical actor-system. Culture System stresses the systems of meanings alone. Personality System then is subordinate to the concept of the Culture System.

CULTURE SYSTEM

↓

Internalized

↓

PERSONALITY SYSTEM

Figure 5

B. FOUR PHASES OF THE PERSONALITY SYSTEM

The systems of need dispositions and internalized culture standards are broken down into four basic types and are compiled under the general title of "orientations to objects" which is shown in the following format:

INTEREST IN INSTRUMENTAL UTILIZATION	CONSUMATORY NEEDS
NEEDS FOR COMMITMENT	NEEDS FOR AFFILIATION

FIGURE 6

1. Interest in Instrumental Utilization

Interest in instrumental utilization means survival. The actor must have internalized systems of need dispositions and their systems of orientation regarding concern with the environment and objects in the situation with a view to simple subsistence. The actor must need to survive in the environment. If there were no such interest, if no such system of need dispositions existed, death would result. Autistic children represent an example of lack of sufficient internalized need disposition to survive in an environment, or even to use the objects in an environment to carry out some goal. Once basic survival is met, the problem of manipulating and attending to the environment spirals up into systems of needs dispositions to succeed and survive in varied situations. The actor can have systems of need dispositions regarding the use of tools, books, and other objects, the economic survival of a business, continued membership in a group, completion of rules, or maintaining relationships, etc. In the concept of Instrumental Utilization there is a system of need dispositions associated with using objects and managing situations to survive at many levels.

2. Consumatory Needs

Consumatory Needs applies to those aspects of systems of need dispositions which involve "relations to objects" which produce rewards or punishments. There is a need attached to having or avoiding objects defined as rewards or punishments. Thus the Indian had to "need" to receive feathers for his brave deeds, he had to "fear" the scorn of the Chief, and desire to wear the marks of a "warrior." If he didn't care about any of these rewards or punishments, he would probably not survive in the tribe. Likewise, a student must need "good grades" and "feel upset" at failure or there will be difficulty in arousing the energy needed to study, listen, think, and direct attention. The actors "need" to have the money given out for work, and they "need" to want the objects that the reward of money can buy. Consumatory Needs deals with typical systems of such need dispositons for an actor-system.

3. Needs for Commitment

Needs for Commitment refers to systems of need dispositions for the development and maintenance of "working" norms and values. The actor has a need to define and identify objects, to learn and accept the ideas and rules of social life, and to find them continually dependable. The actor has to "believe" in the meanings of life and value of the world in which he lives. This not so much a case of seeing objects as rewards (which is related to Consumatory Needs) but a need to know objects are valued, and to have the means of experiencing himself as an esteemed object. The emotional-physical matrix of this level of internalization makes it possible for him to recognize and "experience" the respect of others for himself as well as others. It is also the source of the capacity to show esteem and respect towards other objects -- whether they are physical, cultural or social.

4. Needs for Affiliation

Needs for Affiliation means that a typical actor

has systems of need dispositions toward group membership where there are relationships of support. The actor needs to belong to various groups as a participating member, and needs to cooperate in the ways established by the group. If these need dispositions are not present, there will be insufficient motivation or energy to conform to group demands. For a member to maintain a group affiliation, he must feel it is important to belong to that group. Thus if a desire to belong to a fraternity is not firmly fixed in the emotional-physical matrix of a young college man, he may hardly be able to bring himself to swallow goldfish or endure the "humiliations" of initiation rites.

The Personality System is thus defined as a System of orientations and motivations which are **internalized** into the physical-emotional matrix of a typical actor system, and as such are systems of need dispositions.

III. THE SOCIAL SYSTEM

Using the Elements of Action, the Social System abstracts out "ways of doing," or patterns of processes of interactive relationships that obtain between various actor systems. A social system is essentially an **interactive network of relationships.**

A. ROLES

The term normally used to describe the basic unit of a social system is role relationship. The concept of role answers the questions, "**what** is done?," "**how** is it done?," and "**who** should do it?" As such, social systems are considered systems of interrelated roles of actor systems, and this is the case in the General Theory of Action.

However, there is an important difference in the meaning of the term "role" in the General Theory of Action and that used in the general in the general sociological literature. In many sociological discussions the idea of role includes a "meaning" aspect, the role activities, and the appropriate "motivations." Thus the role of "minister" is often described as representing someone who believes in God, who preaches, marries people, cares for the sick and dying, loves people, and wants to do good. The General Theory of Action separates out the aspects of this definition into Culture System, the system of meanings, Social System, the system of role activities, and the Personality System, the system of need dispositions and motivations. Social System in the General Theory of Action only refers to the systems as role activities, and composites of roles of actor systems. **The role is a unit of procedures and ways of behaving that is interrelated to other roles in Social Systems.**

1. Reciprocal Role Systems

It is important to keep in mind the **reciprocal** element of role systems, for it is that part of the "doing" which is most important to the Social System. "Ways of doing" alone are not the **only** element of the Social System. Rather there are "ways of doing" which are **matched** with reciprocal "ways of doing" on the part of other role systems. It is part of the role of minister to preach, and it is part of the role of parishioner to listen. It is the role of boss to direct the work of the section manager, whose job it is to carry out those directions by ordering materials, submitting reports, and organizing the work to be done in that section. Each role is involved in a whole **matrix** of other roles which are set up as constellations which compose Social Systems.

2. Coordinated Role Systems

Such networks of reciprocal systems of expected behaviors also involve systems of **coordination** of performances and responses. The coordinating jobs of supervising, organizing other roles, decision making, and managing are also an integral part of a Social System. They too are roles, and they are intertwined with many other roles.

3. Role Expectations

Reciprocity in roles includes the element of role expectations -- expectations of performances by a certain role incumbent in certain situations. These expectations include those of the actor system of certain performances to be carried out by the actor; certain performances and responses to be carried out by the alter. Expectations are mutual, and it is these networks of mutual expectations of what an actor is expected to **do** in a given situation which constitute a Social System.

a.) Sanctions. As part of role expectations, sanctions represent the **prescribed positive and negative responses** to be given by an actor in response to types of action by an alter. When an action is carried out correctly, there is a set of role behaviors to be used to recognize this. Grades are a good example for it is the job of the teacher role to respond to the work of a student by means of grade sanctions -- either good or bad. Giving out grades is built into the teacher role system.

b.) Norms. Expectations which are **standards or conditions** are called norms. Such expectations serve as measures and criteria for performances, and thus are the basis for what sanctions will be carried out. Norms can be informal or formal. They can be tentative and only vaguely spelled out or they can be codified in rigidly designed rules and laws. All expectations, then, have a normative element to them.

When two friends start to carry out a job together, an informal norm that the "younger" will do the heavy work and the "older" do the arranging might evolve. This is normative in the sense that it comes to be expected and a violation would be met by some negative sanction by the older actor. At the other extreme, if an actor-company makes a contract with a city government to build a bridge for a prescribed amount of money and by a certain time, the violation of any one of these expectations could result in a legal suit being filed by alter, possible arrest of company officers, and termination of the right to carry out business. The sanctions here are written in the law and are quite specific.

4. Status

Status indicates the **positional aspect of a role** in a Social System -- where the role is "located" in the Social System relative to other roles. This location is called "status," or the place in the relationship system. Thus the role of college president is located "above" that of teacher or student, and has more "status." This status-role" bundle is not one of general attributes of an actor but is a unit of a Social System.

The concept of role as a component of Social Systems includes networks of reciprocal expectations or norms with varying levels of formality.

It is important to remember that a role is not an actor. The concept of actor belongs to the first level of abstraction, the Elements of Action. Culture System, Social System and Personality System are all abstracted from the single concept of the actor in a situation, and so it follows that Social Systems represent only **one** aspect of the concept actor, namely patterns of ways of doing and behaving. Meaning systems and motive systems are not included in the Social System because they are represented by the concepts of Culture System and Personality System.

B. TOTAL SYSTEMS AND SUB-SYSTEMS

1. Society

The largest unit of a Social System is usually

considered a "society." Here the designating factor is that the total system as defined can be treated as self-subsisting, meaning that approximately all the functional performance systems required to keep the system going and together are included within its boundaries.

But societies do not **exist** as such. "Society" is simply another abstraction which refers only to a type of Social System which is also a theoretical construction. Sweaty people really alive and moving are **not** the primary component units of a Social System. **Roles** are. Role does not stand for actor, but for systems of reciprocal expectations of actors. Sub-systems are also simply systems of roles or expected performances organized to carry out some goal. So the concept society could refer to the systems of institutions in the United States which include business, government, fraternities, and marriage composed of sub-systems of roles.

2. Institution

The concept institution refers to a **composite system of interdependent roles which is of strategic significance to a given Social System.** Institutions should not be confused with collectivities. A collectivity is a system of concretely interactive specific actors. An institution is a complex of patterned elements of role-expectations which may apply to an indefinite number of collectivities. Thus it is possible to speak of the "institution of property" in a Social System which brings together all the aspects of roles which have to do with governing the definitions of rights and obligations related to "possessions."

To summarize these aspects of Social Systems, the following chart may be helpful:

Action = system of action

Norms = standards of expected behavior

Roles = clusters of norms focused upon a specific function

Institutions = clusters of roles of strategic significance to a social system

Society = Composite of institutions that is fairly self sufficient

C. INSTITUTIONALIZATION

Institutionalization represents the process whereby actor systems translate cultural values and ideas into ways of doing and interacting. It is the way values become organized into systems of action. It is the doing part of meaning systems. If a high school senior keeps talking of the importance of higher education, people will expect to see an application to some colleges.

Meanings systems which are institutionalized in social systems are also "internalized" in the Personality System. In this case the meanings, values and beliefs are incorporated into the emotional matrix of the character structure of a typical actor so that the actor "wants" to carry out the role prescriptions and act in the ways which carry out the beliefs. If this process of institutionalization and internalization has not taken place, or has developed severe contradictions, the actor will not act in the established ways and the cultural meaning is not actualized or viable. The conveniences, comforts, and rewards of the society will not be sufficiently valued to cause people to undertake and obtain them by their own efforts. The "system" of that society would founder in confusion, disruption or for a lack of partakers.

In recalling the theoretical character of each system concept, and recognizing that each of the three systems represents but an aspect of a whole situation, internalization and institutionalization fall into their logical context. If an actor system is the primary unit of study, and action (relationships) is approached from three different points of view, it would not be possible to think of any one of the three systems as separate or independent from the others. An action system equals "meaning system" - "motive system" - "doing system."

One final comment needs to be made about the relationship of the Culture System to the Personality and Social Systems. Culture has a special quality of "transmissibility" that is not present in Personality System or Social System. A value can pass from one action system to another, yet nothing is "taken away" from the original system. Nothing is "lost." Yet there is a "gain" in the inclusion of the new value into a different system. It is this characteristic of transmissibility that makes the Culture System the least "empirical," and hence the most abstract. Action patterns are considered more directly traceable than the ideas that motivate them. You can "see" one man punch another, but you cannot "see" why he did so. On the level of the Personality System it is possible to measure blood pressure, heart rate, and other indications of the physical-emotional matrix in action, but you cannot measure the motives that give rise to the physical expressions. The punch may be a gesture of affection in some groups, an indication of anger in others. For one person it is coolly if not coldly rendered while for another it is an explosion of emotion. The aspect of culture, then, is more remote from the Situation of Action than ways of acting or behavior patterns.

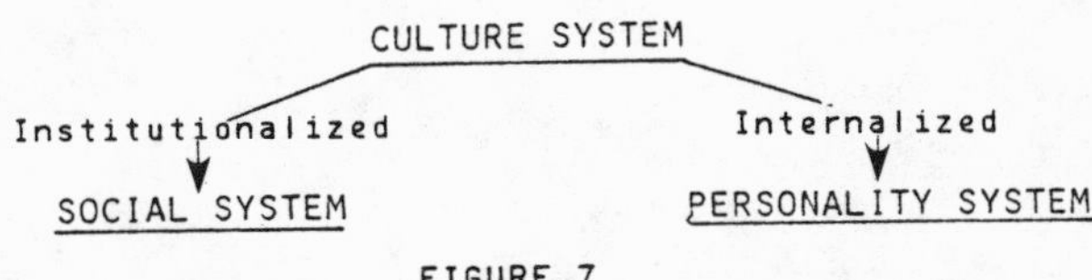

FIGURE 7

D. FOUR PHASES OF SOCIAL SYSTEMS

As was the case with the previous two action systems, i.e., Culture and Personality Systems, there are four phases to any Social System. These are shown in Figure 8:

ADAPTIVE	GOAL ATTAINMENT
LATENT PATTERN MAINTENANCE	INTEGRATIVE

FIGURE 8

These systems will be discussed in the next chapter as the "A-G-I-L."

5

"A-G-I-L": THE SYSTEM OF ACTION

The next level of the General Theory of Action sees a System of Action as having four phases abstracted from the three systems of Culture System, Social System and Personality System (Plate I). The implication is that any system of action has certain common theoretical characteristics which always apply to any type or level of action system. Since the Culture System, Social System and Personality System are all systems of action, it follows that they will have similar features characteristic of all systems of action. The "System of Action" is a more general concept than the Culture System, Social System, or Personality System. This would be similar to the idea that the concept "matter," or any substance which occupies space and has weight, is the more general concept with "liquid matter" and "solid matter" as sub-types. Both liquid matter and solid matter have characteristics in common, (they occupy space and have weight) which permit them to fit into the category of matter in general, yet as sub-categories, they have characteristics which distinguish them from each other. Liquid matter takes the shape of its container, and solid matter has a definite volume and shape. Other examples would have "human being" or "bird" as the general category and "male/female" or "duck, eagle, robin, or wren" as some of the sub-categories. In the General Theory of Action, System of Action is the general category and Culture System, Social System, and Personality System as sub-categories. They are all systems of action, however as sub-types, Culture System, Social System, and Personality System have other features which distinguish them from each other. This is demonstrated in Plate IV.

Plate IV shows the System of Action with four phases or aspects, the A, G, I, and L. Since these four phases are characteristic of **all** systems of action, they are the main theoretical device used to compare, contrast, and analyze relationships in and between various sub-systems in order to generate hypotheses.

Before starting the discussion of the System of Action and its four phases, it is necessary to define some concepts which are crucial to an explanation of the phases; namely **Function** and **Environment.** Each of these terms has a unique meaning in the General Theory of Action which is incompatible with the usual definitions used.

I. PRELIMINARY DEFINITIONS

A. FUNCTION

In sociology the term "function" has had a turbulent history accompanied by volumes of debate where different scholars have very different if not conflicting definitions of the term. These different interpretations can consequently transform the implications of an idea in its theoretical context. To read a work with a meaning at great variance with the author's original intent can result in a vast misunderstanding.

In the General Theory of Action, the term function has special reference to "systems." The word function is defined as an **output** from one system to another. There is a "delivery" to one system from another system, and hence a function has **direction.** Using the example of a circuit diagram again, the "function" of a diode is an "output" to a resistor. In mathematics, the "function" of the symbol "+" is that it contributes an "output" or delivery into a number system: 1 + 3 = 4. Functions can be thought of as "conceptual bridges between theoretical systems."7

The bridge or function should **NOT** be thought of as an "effect." The "+" is not the answer. The "+" is only the delivery, the message, not the result or the effect. A function is a message that is "output" and received between systems, and not the consequence of the interaction. Function can also be thought of as "mediation" between systems which is "internuncial." In Latin the term internuncial uses the base of "inter" meaning "between," and "nuncius" which means messenger, resulting in the idea of a "messenger between" systems. When the term function is used then, it means "messenger," "bridge," or "output" between theoretical systems.

The concept of function entails the complimentary idea of **input** or reception of the message. If a message is not received, it does not complete itself **as** a message. If a bridge does not go the whole way across a span, it does not serve (or function) as a bridge. A function, or output is a two-way concept that requires reception or input for completion.

Not all "functions" are received by all target systems. What comes "into" a system is controlled by the characteristics of that system. For example the function "+" works in mathematical systems, but would not work in a musical system. How would you "play" a "+" or "%"?

In another case, a communications satellite used in space is designed to process sound signals or "beeps." These are sent and received by computers which transform letters and vocal sounds into the beeps, and reconfigure them upon reception to be printed out on paper or broadcast over television. The "function" of the sender system is the "beeps." The receiver system is designed to accept these "beeps" by its "informational mechanisms." If the computer which is sending the signal malfunctions and sends hums instead of beeps the receiver system will either reject the hums as irrelevant input or it might transform the hums by recording them as beeps and the printout would be jibberish.

Remembering that a system of action is a system of relationships, a function represents a relationship with output on one end that is sent, and input on the other that is received.

The formal definition of function in the General Theory of Action is: **an energetic output of an action system into another system, controlled informationally by the adaptive mechanisms of that receptor system.**[8]

B. ENVIRONMENT

Most people think of the "out-of-doors" as the environment -- trees, ocean, sky, hills, noise, or smog. In the General Theory of Action this is not the case. "Environment" in the General Theory of Action refers to "systems." The "environment" of one system is another system. Environment is the "interface," or the area of contact, of one system to another -- the boundary of one system that touches another as it is diagrammed. Interface and boundary are determined by the way the systems are theoretically constructed, and the point of reference chosen by the theorist.

For example, let us say that "five" is a system. It represents 1,1,1,1,1. Let us also say that "six" is a system, seven a system, etc. These systems are part of the larger number system: 1, 2, 3, 4, 5, 6, 7, 8, 9, 10. The "environment" of the system "five" would be "four" and "six." The "environment" of "seven" is "six" and "eight." In the following example, each cell represents a sub-system of the larger whole system:

	a	b	c	d	e	
	f	g	h	i	j	

FIGURE 9

The environment of cell "c" will be the systems that interface, or act as boundaries to that cell: or "b," "h," and "d." If the cells were arranged differently, the "environments" would be different. The terms Environment and Function are both relative, depending on the relationships between various systems.

In Plate VII the environment of the cell showing the "A" system is "L" and "G." The environment of "L" is "A" and "I," etc.

II. FUNCTIONAL PREREQUISITES OF SYSTEMS

Functional prerequisites (Plate IV) are **imperatives for system survival.** They are **outputs** or "functions" of a system which are **required** if that system is to continue to survive as a system in its "environment." The given system **has to** deliver certain outputs which must be received by environment or boundary systems, and it must receive inputs from that environment system if it is to persist or develop in an orderly fashion as a system in its environment.

For example, a gasoline engine must give off exhaust fumes or it will explode. Humans must breathe or they will die. A long distance runner must perspire, and so on. Analogously, systems must generate functions into their environment, which also must be able to receive them if they are to survive. On another level, IBM Research Division is designed to do research on computers which is to be received by the larger company for development and sales. If the Research Division begins to turn out paintings, comic strips, or jokes, it is not hard to imagine what would happen to the Division Manager and a number of subordinate personnel. The same thing would happen if the Division provided no output at all to the company.

A. TYPES OF PREREQUISITES

In the General Theory of Action there are two types of Prerequisites: Universal and Structural.

A **Universal Prerequisite** is one that includes a whole system surviving in relation to its environment. A **Structural Prerequisite** is one that refers to the successful functioning of the component parts of a whole system relative to each other. If the environment is thought of as external to a system, then the universal prerequisite is met when there is a functional interchange with the external boundary systems. The structural prerequisites are met when the internal functions of the systems are working.

Using IBM as an example again, it is possible to talk of the survival of IBM as a whole system in its environment of the modern world as the Universal Imperative. Structural Prerequisites would include the relationship of the various divisions of IBM to each other: Accounting to Management, Research to Production, Production to Management, etc. If Management does not convey to Production the specifications for orders, or Sales does not have information about what products are being developed, there would be a serious problem in the maintenance of the Structural Prerequisites. To show how relative the idea ot Functional Prerequisites is, it would be possible to determine that the Research Department is the whole system under study. Its "environment" becomes the rest of IBM, the Government, customers, etc., and the Structural Prerequisites would include the Research sub-divisions of Planning, Pure Research, Physics, Software, Management, etc.

An example of a breakdown of these systems can be shown in two ways. A modern singing group usually involves an organization of the singers and those who manage their tours, contracts, etc. The Beatles, as a system of action, showed that they met the universal prerequisite of selling records, booking tours, etc. However, their structural imperative was not met. The group could not generate internal functional relationships that permitted ongoing success, and they finally broke up. In an opposite case, you can imagine a very cohesive refugee family coming to the United States and opening a restaurant. They do not speak the language and do not know anyone in their city who speaks their language. The structural prerequisites are met very well. However, they are unable to understand or meet the health codes, the tax and legal requirements of the city, etc. They are unable to adhere to the universal prerequisites in the functional interchange with the environment and they are forced to close down.

Plate V shows the four functional prerequisites of the System of Action. These four prerequisites are generally represented in a four-cell system or square as shown. The prerequisites are: **ADAPTION,** usually referred to as the "A" Phase which fulfills the universal prerequisite; **GOAL ATTAINMENT** usually referred to as the "G" Phase; **INTEGRATION** usually referred to as the "I" Phase; and **LATENT PATTERN MAINTENANCE** usually referred to as the "L" Phase, all of which fit the structural prerequisite. It is the contention of the General Theory of Action that the types of functions (system outputs) represented by these four phases **MUST** be carried out in any system of action if the system is to survive. However the relative importance and the relationship to each other may vary a great deal.

1. ADAPTIVE

Every system of action must develop and maintain some scheme of adaptive outputs to the environment which are received by that environment if it is to survive in that environment. This pattern of adaption (Adaptive or A Phase) represents the Universal Imperative. It is the special character of the A Phase to focus upon the purely functional problems of coping and surviving in the external environment.

Adaptive functions are those which deal with **patterns of interchange with the external environmental systems.** They are the processes of producing outputs which can be used by the system in order to continue as a system in that environment.

A case of such adaption would develop in the case of actors stranded on a strange, uninhabited island. In order to survive, they must create ways of coping with the new and strange environment. Figuring out ways of finding and identifying edible food is of paramount importance for they would all die otherwise. Shelter must be constructed to protect against the winds and rain. Tools must be developed to carry out the jobs involved in survival and a system of direction is needed for the management of those jobs. The people must solve the Universal Imperative of Adaptation -- they must contrive outputs to that environmental system in which they find themselves that will be received, and hence permit them to survive.

In another example, if you go to Europe with a hair dryer or electric shaver, you need an adaptor, since the electrical current is different in many of those countries. Your appliance would not work properly in that system, and in fact might overload. The appliance systems must have some mechanism for interfacing with the foreign electrical systems or else they will not work. They must be capable of adapting to the environmental systems, just as the refugee family must adapt if it is to survive as a restaurant system.

The Adaptive Phase represents the "business" and "work" of a System of Action. In the Western world the whole range of business is engaged in ways of providing for adaption and survival on many levels, and with high degrees of sophistication. Agriculture, transportation, communications, finance, and service are only a few of the industries that are engaged in the function of system and member survival.

2. LATENT PATTERN MAINTENANCE

Once a system has developed a mode of survival in boundary environments, it must next develop the means of ensuring the continuance of those patterns. The total System of Action, including both the Culture

System and the Social System has to be "passed on" and it must be maintained as "worthwhile." People must come to understand it, believe it, and find the renunciations required of them legitimate. They must have some means of finding stability in their expectations and some means of fulfillment. They must be socialized into the Culture System and Social System. This is the function of the Latent Pattern Maintenance Phase.

The term "Latent" is used here because these patterns are often dormant. They need to be learned so that when the proper situation arises, they can be used. People are not always tempted to cheat. However, when the opportunity arises, the values about not cheating are remembered and used.

Continuing with the example of the actors stranded on the island, we can expect they will share the new ideas they have, the technical lore they have designed, and these will be passed on to the babies that no doubt will be born. It is vital that the babies as new members be initiated into the working System of Action so they will know what it is and how to get along with it. They must be socialized into these on-going systems, and thus a system for passing on the Adaptive, Integrative, and Goal Attainment systems must come about. In this way there will be a provision for the replacement and maintenance of role systems. The Latent Pattern Maintenance System then is a socialization system. It represents a structured plan for the initiation of new units or members into the System of Action already developed. It provides for a viable communication system between members. By means of the Latent Pattern Maintenance System, all phases of language are learned, and the Culture and Social Systems are passed on.

If the socialization process does not take place, or is not successful, the larger system will experience stress. Thus, if students do not learn the skills required to work and live in their society, such as reading, writing, and math skills, as well as other areas of competence, the society loses useful members and the students are frustrated and unsuccessful in getting along. On a smaller scale, you probably would not want to be operated on by a doctor who cheated his way through medical school, or fly in a plane designed by someone who cheated his way through an aerospace engineering degree. The society functions when its members are competent in their skills. The airlines would be hard pressed to do business if their aircraft were unreliable. Even the military depends on a high level of competence today because of the need to read complex technical manuals and use sophisticated equipment. If the recruits are not competent, if the Latent Pattern Maintenance system is not functional, the military will not be capable of meeting an attack successfully, and the society will not be able to continue to carry on its Adaptive System for surviving and maintining a functional interchange with its environment.

The Latent Pattern Maintenance System has the additional function of "tension management" or constant reintorcement ot the results of socialization. It has to keep the members happy to live by its values and standards. In this way the participating units will find the efforts required to keep the system going "worth it" in spite ot the difficulties involved. Thus, once a student elects not to cheat, he needs to know it was the right thing to do even though no one else knows of the decision or the struggle. This can come through the media, at his church or temple, from teachers, politicans, authors, etc. who testify subtly or directy about the value and importance of honesty. The same applies to standards used in the system of action fundamental to work, daily living, school, and home. There is always tension, temptation, and difficulty in daily life. These can be endured, the tension managed, if there is sufficient support generated for living by those values, and if there is recognized meaning attached to the effort.

3. INTEGRATION

Every System of Action, with its patterns of survival and patterns of socialization and tension management, must also have some **means of social control.** Patterns of coordination and cooperation must be set up so that problems of deviant behavior by actors can be handled in such a way as not to destroy the total system.

On the island laws, rules, enforcement techniques, and legitimate bodies to carry out these functions need to be established. It is inevitable that some of the members of the group will be disruptive. In order to keep such disturbances within safe limits, and to protect both system members as well as the system as a whole, rules must be developed and patterns of social control must evolve along with systems of coordination and definitions of deviance. In this way the solidarity of the total system is maintained by the defining, checking and removal of disruptive interference with the system while the conditions of harmonious cooperation are promoted. (The General Theory of Action does not suggest that systems **should** be maintained without disruption. It holds that **if** a system is to continue "as is," it requires sufficient social control.)

In another example, circuit breakers are used to control excess or "wandering" energy. Even computers have "control" systems which identify wayward data and redirect or remove them into some residual category so that they do not interfere with the rest of the computer functions.

Integrative mechanisms function to "integrate" system units by maintaining cooperative and harmonious solidarity.

4. GOAL ATTAINMENT

The final Structural Imperative deals with the definition and assignment of power. This system is involved in the identification of which functions benefit the System of Action and defining reward functions. There must be some agreed upon rewards and punishments as well as a means to identify the source of power. By specifying facilities (possessions which are significant as means to other goals) and rewards there is a mobilization of the capacity of the system to obtain system goals, and interchange within the system is made possible.

On the island, the actors have decided that pieces of bark are to be used as "money" or the main type of exchange to be used as facilities for goods and services. Consequently the person with the most bark may have more power than those with less bark. Working for the bark makes it possible to have other rewards such as nice furniture or better food. In another case the people may find that having the job of agriculture manager is also a facility for it gives access to and control over the distribution of essential food. Such status facilities are also examples of "possessions." Such transferable facilities involve "bundles of rights" that involve certain expected behavior and attitudes that may lead to a reward that distinguishes the person in that position by more elegant treatment.

Rewards on the island will be desired objects of immediate gratification either as a physical object or in some relationship to the perspective of the actor. Receiving a wreath of seaweed may be seen as a reward for bravery by an islander. Buying a fine meal, nice clothes, or a prime beach home are rewards that come from the use of bark money or facilities.

The process of exchange and designation of authority status come together to permit the definition of power, or what Parsons often refers to as "polity" in a System of Action. Power on the social system level is defined in the General Theory of Action as "the capacity of a social system to mobilize resources to attain collective goals."[9] The generation of this power takes place through the ordering of statuses, authority and the regulation of private activities. The facilities and reward systems make it possible to mobilize "resources" so that social goals can be obtained. Thus as people work for facilities and seek (and believe in) culturally defined rewards, the resources of the society are ordered and mobilized to make it possible for that society to function. On an actor system level, the facilities and rewards also provide "means" to "future goods" and thus also constitute a type of power. The Functional Imperative met in the Goal Attainment Phase is the **mobilization of the necessary prerequisites for the attainment of system goals** through designation and the system of exchanges involved in facilities and rewards which lead to wealth and power.

Summing up the Universal and Structural Imperatives, we have the following:

Universal Prerequisite:
Adaption

Structural Prerequisites:
Latent Pattern Maintenance
Integrative
Goal Attainment

The whole system must survive in the "environment" and to do this, it must develop patterns of interchange with the environment as functional outputs received by that environment. It must have an Adaptive system. Given this Adaptive system, it must have means of maintaining the system of adaption by socialization and tension management (Latent Pattern Maintenance Phase); it must control disruptive elements and promote cooperation (Integrative Phase); and it must define and provide facilities, rewards, and power to permit exchange which make possible the attainment of system goals (Goal Attainment Phase). The L,I, and G Phases deal with the structural continuance of the system as a whole and are focused **within** the system, while the A Phase centers on the exchange **outside** the system and the interface of the system as a whole with its environment. If the structure of the internal system functions properly it will be irrelevant if the total system cannot successfully survive in its environment. Likewise, if the system can accomplish its interchange with its environment but is not coordinated within, it will not be able to maintain the pattern of adaptation and eventually will not be able to continue to produce the functions which enable it to survive in its environment. It will collapse.

III. PHASE QUALITIES

Each of the four phases has a special set of qualities (see Plate VI) that correspond to the functions of that phase. There is a different set of qualities for each of the four phases. Since each of the functions of each phase represents some prerequisite it follows that the qualities associated with each phase will also have an imperative aspect. Not only must the phase functions be produced by the systems, but they must be carried out in a particular way.

1. Adaptive Quality

It is not enough to plant seeds in a field for them to grow and survive. It is necessary that the planting be done in a technically efficient way. If the farmer puts the seeds in a steel box and plants them, they will not grow. If there is no sunshine, or too much in that area, the seeds may die. If there is no water, most seeds will never even sprout. Different seeds require specialized environments, and the farmer must know this if he depends on his harvest to survive.

This example of technical efficiency applies to the Adaptive Phase where the functional prerequisite is the production of outputs which will interchange with the external environment in such a way that the system will survive. The **Quality** of those outputs, or the way in which the functions are discharged, must be one of **technical efficiency**, or the functions will not be successful. Hence, the farmer who takes his whole sack of seeds and puts them all on top of a rock to admire their colors and shapes may think he has planted the seeds, but they will not grow. Neither will the french fries or dollar bills he planted lovingly in the ground. The environmental systems of growth are inconsistent with the **way** in which the function was delivered to that system. The function of Adaption must be accompanied by the quality of technical efficiency. Seeds must be planted, and they must be planted in the proper method.

This quality of technical competence also applies to computers. It is not enough to input information or data into a computer. The data must be conveyed to the computer in a precise way and sequence. The programmer must be technically efficient or the printout will be a mass of meaningless symbols.

2. Latent Pattern Maintenance Quality

The functional prerequisite of the Latent Pattern Maintenance Phase is socialization and tension management. The **Quality** of this phase is **cultural value commitment.** Not only must the systems of the society be passed on, but they must be passed on in such a manner that they are received. The socializing agent has to be in concurrence with the System of Action, and cannot be against it. The **right** system must be passed on and in the proper perspective.

In the school it is not enough for the teacher to teach students. If the System of Action is to be maintained, the teacher must educate in accordance with the larger System of Action so that the students will not only learn to accept it, but believe and follow it. The system must be conducive to the student internalization of the larger system. To do otherwise would be a, significant threat to the larger system because it would lose replacement actors and those actors who did work in the system might not perform according to the prescribed norms. This would constitute a danger in that the students -- or new system members -- would not be able to perform successfully in the system. The system would then lack the means of continuance because it could not produce the required functions to survive in the environment. Teachers, then, must be committed to the system values and procedures. If they teach revolutionary ideas and ways of behaving, or if they do not teach the skills members need to function in the larger system, the students will not be able to fit into the already going society which can prove very troublesome for them and injurious to the society.

If a computer programmer is taught Basic as a computer language when the computer to be used requires Fortran, the programmer's efforts will be defective. The teacher must be committed to teaching the language used on the computer the programmer will work on if that programmer is to have any success.

<u>3. Integrative Quality</u>

The function of the Integrative Phase is social control and coordination. The **Quality** of the Integrative Phase is **loyalty.** The agents responsible for coordination and control must be **loyal** to the larger System of Action, coordinating efforts to help the larger system function effectively, and suppress any acts or systems that would inhibit that goal. Such coordination acts to integrate the system as a whole, giving a "fair" opportunity for all legitimate interests through enforcement, and legislation.

A police officer who belongs to the Mafia will not be able to be loyal to the larger society. He will be loyal to the Mafia, and will constitute a threat to the functioning of the larger system because he will not control those who violate its norms and laws. If a large number of officers were members of the Mafia, laws could not be enforced and the larger system would be in danger of collapse.

<u>4. Goal Attainment Quality</u>

The function of the Goal Attainment Phase is to facilitate interchange within the system by means of facilities, rewards and the definition of power.

The **Quality** of the Goal Attainment Phase is the **legitimation of system or unit goals.** This means that there must be acceptable objects to be used as exchange and rewards, and facilities must be given for activities which support the function of the larger System of Action. Goals are made achievable and believable through the rewards and facilities which help to bring them about.

If it is the job of General Motors to build cars for the nation's transportation system, enough money must be paid to workers and management to get that job done. Workers and managers must desire the money and the kinds of rewards it and their status will provide. Those who build better cars more efficiently will receive more facilities, have access to more rewards, and thus gain power. Power will then come to those most in accord with system goals. If the General Motors staff do not want the rewards, or the facilities will not bring wished-for rewards, the people will not work, and the job will not be done. If facilities and rewards are given for non-goal related activities, like being nice to the boss, or dressing neatly, or writing nice poetry, those most able to do the job will not be promoted, and again, the goal will not be obtained. This is the way all the goals of the larger System of Action are furthered, and the way in which power is achieved and wielded.

The quality involved in General Motors means that actors are not only rewarded, but they can use those rewards to obtain other hoped-for situations or objects. The facilities and rewards act as an exchange system. Many goals are rewarded with money, and the money can be exchanged for any number of varied objects and services produced by the system. The money then serves as a fluid mechanism which keeps the whole system functioning. The facilities and rewards then legitimize the over-all system goals.

The second Goal Attainment Quality of System Goal Commitment will be explained in the section on phase emphasis toward the end of the chapter.

IV. SUB SYSTEMS OF THE GENERAL THEORY OF ACTION

Looking back to Plate IV, it can be seen that each of the three systems developed earlier, Culture System, Social System, and Personality System has four phases. Therefore there will be patterns of Adaption in each of the three systems, patterns for Latent Pattern Maintenance, patterns for Integration, and patterns for Goal Attainment.

For the Culture System this means that there will be patterns of systems of meanings with four sub-types: there will be meanings which are basically Adaptive in that they are related to the **meaning** of survival in that system; patterns of meanings which fill the Latent Pattern Maintenance function of existential interpretation of the ground of meaning for the whole system; patterns of meanings related to the function of Integration or the moral evaluative definitions of right and wrong; and finally patterns of meanings related to Goal Attainment, or the meanings of rewards, facilities, power, etc. These four phases of the Culture System were initially discussed as sub-categories of the Culture System. Actually, they represent the Four Phases of the System of Action on the Culture System level. They would now look like this:

THE CULTURE SYSTEM

ADAPTIVE PHASE	GOAL ATTAINMENT
COGNITIVE SYMBOLIZATION	EXPRESSIVE SYMBOLIZATION
LATENT PATTERN MAINTENANCE	INTEGRATIVE
EXISTENTIAL INTERPRETATION	MORAL EVALUATIVE CATEGORIZATION

FIGURE 10

On the Personality System level, the four phases again apply. There is an Adaptive Phase of Need Dispositions which involve interest in and needs to manipulate the environment in order to survive. On the Latent Pattern Maintenance level there are systems of Need Dispositions to believe and hold values. On the Integrative level, there are Need Dispositions to belong to the group and be accepted as a member. Finally, on the Goal Attainment level, there are systems of Need Dispositions related to the consumption of certain objects as rewards and the attainment of other objects as facilities. The Four Phase diagram of the System of Action on the Personality System level is as follows:

PERSONALITY SYSTEM

ADAPTIVE PAHSE	GOAL ATTAINMENT
INTEREST IN INSTRUMENTAL UTILIZATION	CONSUMMATORY NEEDS
LATENT PATTERN MAINTENANCE	INTEGRATIVE
NEEDS FOR COMMITMENT	NEEDS FOR AFFILIATION

FIGURE 11

On the Social System level, the case is the same, and the four phases deal with ways of acting. Thus there are patterns of interchange with the environment which are Adaptive. There are patterns of socialization which involve Latent Pattern Maintenance. There are patterns of social control and integration which are Integrative, and there are patterns of ways of allocating rewards and defining objects as facilities or rewards which is the Goal Attainment Phase. The diagram is a follows:

THE SOCIAL SYSTEM

ADAPTIVE	GOAL ATTAINMENT
WAYS OF SURVIVAL Economic Systems	WAYS OF ALLOCATING FACILITIES AND REWARDS Polity
LATENT PATTERN MAINTENANCE	INTEGRATIVE
WAYS OF SOCIALIZATION AND TENSION MANAGEMENT Family, Religious and Educational Systems	WAYS OF SOCIAL CONTROL AND COORDINATION Government and Law Enforcement Systems

FIGURE 12

It is time to pause and re-establish perspective to keep all these ideas in order. The major point is that **any** Action System has four phases. Each of the four phases fills a given function which is necessary to the survival of the system in its environment. Each of these four functions has an accompanying quality which dictates the **way** a function is to be carried out if the functional output is to be successful as a message to another system. Function is the **what** of the relationship, and quality is the **how.** This can be summarized in Figure 13.

The categories of the System of Action can be used on many levels of abstraction -- something like a "zoom lens" of a camera. Its focus can be very wide, or it can close down to a microscopic level -- all depending on the whim and needs of the photographer/theorist. When the lens is wide open, there is a view of Action in its most general sense. Closing down to a medium range and looking **just** at some sub-system, the four phases are still working, but just as they relate to that level of meaning systems or role systems.

ELEMENTS OF THE SYSTEM OF ACTION

PHASE	FUNCTION	QUALITY
ADAPTIVE	INTERCHANGE WITH THE EXTERNAL ENVIRONMENT FOR SURVIVAL	TECHNICAL EFFICIENCY
LATENT PATTERN MAINTENANCE	SOCIALIZATION AND TENSION MANAGE- MENT; COMMITMENT	CULTURAL VALUE
INTEGRATIVE	COORDINATION AND CONTROL	LOYALTY
GOAL ATTAINMENT	ALLOCATION OF FACILITIES AND REWARDS; INTER- CHANGE WITHIN THE SYSTEM	SYSTEM AND/OR UNIT GOAL COMMITMENT

FIGURE 13

Plate VII demonstrates the differentiation in levels of analysis possible within the General Theory of Action. The point of attention in the diagram is the Latent Pattern Maintenance Phase, but the same principles hold for all the system levels. The example shows that the L Phase itself can be looked at in terms of all four phases, and within each phase, it is possible to break down the system into four phases, on and on.

As an example, let us look at the Latent Pattern Maintenance Phase on the Social System level. Here the primary function is socialization and tension management. The roles related to these functions are usually those associated with institutions of education, religion, parenthood, etc. Now, if the focus is placed on educational systems, we find there are aspects of those role systems directly related to socialization such as teaching, but there are also other aspects such as the Adaptive functions which must be met in dealing with the environmental systems of the school. This can include the school building, relationships with school board officials, government officials, food, supply systems, etc., all functions carried out by the principal.

The Integrative aspect of organization of the socialization process and social control of deviance must be met both in terms of students as well as the staff, and on the Goal Attainment level, there must be some allocation and definition of facilities and rewards for students and teachers, etc. Next, the Adaptive system of the role of the principal's office can also be looked at from the perspective of the whole System of Action and its four phases. Thus, the principal must socialize the maintenance crew or new staff who come to work in the office (Latent Pattern Maintenance Phase). This role entails coordination of maintenance, supply ordering, food services, reporting, etc., and none of these operations can get out of control with pilferage, mistakes, etc. (Integrative Phase). There must be a system of rewards to get all these operations carried out, which involves the Goal Attainment Phase. All of these are simply aspects of the Adaptive roles of the principal in an L Phase educational system. The same can be done for the classroom systems, etc.

The possibilities for changing and extending the levels of analysis are endless, yet the fundamental device for analysis is simple -- the four phases of the System of Action. The complexity of the General Theory of Action does not lie in its tools, but in the levels of analysis that can be explored with these tools and the levels and types of comparison and contrast that can be developed. It is **IMPERATIVE** in doing an analysis, however, that the levels are kept clearly identified to avoid confusion.

V. PHASE EMPHASIS

In any System of Action there will always be **one** phase which is emphasized to a greater degree than the others, and this is shown in Figure 14.

PHASE EMPHASIS

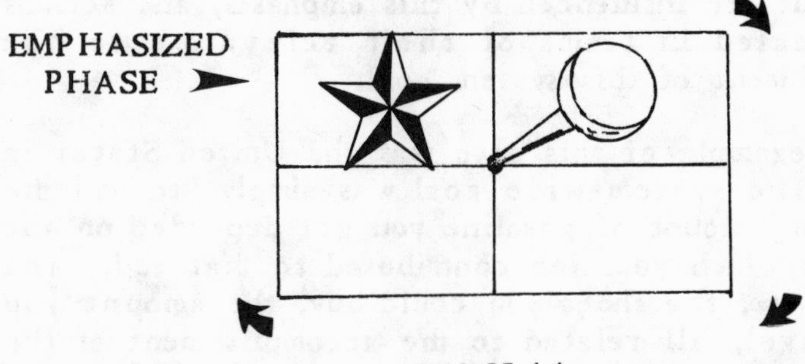

FIGURE 14

The phase to be emphasized is placed in the upper left hand corner of the four cells, and any one of the four phases can appear there. However, the **sequence** of the four phases must always remain the same. Thus the L Phase could appear in the upper left cell, but the I would be directly under it, the A in the upper right cell, and the G in the lower right cell. If the whole set of four cells is thought of with a pin in the center which permits the whole block to move so that different cells can appear in the upper right hand corner, the sequence is preserved. The boundaries of the cells always remain the same, and each cell will always be in the same position **relative** to the other cells.

The purpose in phase emphasis is to indicate the relative importance associated with certain functions in specific societies or sub-systems. Thus in education the L Phase should predominate, whereas in business the A Phase functions are overruling. In law enforcement, government, etc., the I Phase functions are strongest.

In the special case where the Goal Attainment Phase is in the "system goal attainment" mode the significance of the G Phase changes and has a concomitant influence on the rest of the System of Action. In this case the G Phase is predominant (in the top right corner cell). What is peculiar to this state is that the total System of Action is characterized by a common, **specific** attainable goal recognized by all the actors of the system. All actions carried out are influenced by this emphasis, and actions are evaluated in terms of their relevance to the accomplishment of this system goal.

An example of this case was the United States in WW II. The system-wide goal was simply "to win the war". The amount of gasoline you got depended on the degree to which your job contributed to that end. The food you ate, the shoes you could buy, the amount you could travel, all related to the accomplishment of the goal. Children and adults collected lard, papers, and other war related materials. Parents with sons or daughters in the military hung in their windows red, white and blue banners with blue stars for each child serving. If they died, the blue was replaced with gold. Everything that was done was evaluated against this overarching standard: "win the war". The prestige of war related efforts was a primary facility and reward.

This situation contrasts starkly with that of the Vietnam War. In that case the United States was predominately Adaptive Phase with values of business and individual success prevailing. Money was the major facility and rewards were material objects produced by the business sector. A lifetime was to be judged against a series of technical accomplishments. To die at eighteen with no opportunity to prove oneself was not easily understandable. In a society where every technical means is used to preserve life so people can pursue individual success, a preventable death in an unpopular war was very difficult for many to accept, and many refused. The General Theory of Action would see this as a comparison between the United States during WW II as a society in G Phase, and the United States during the Vietnam Conflict in an A Phase. For further elaboration of this point see the chart on "Characteristics of Societies According of System Phase Emphasis".

CHARACTERISTICS OF SOCIETIES ACCORDING TO SYSTEM PHASE EMPHASIS

I. A PHASE

(UNIVERSALISTIC-PERFORMANCE SOCIETY)
EXAMPLE: THE U.S.A.

Cognitive versus expressive.
Individualistic.
Pluralism of goals -- unity of direction rather than content.
Focus on occupational goals, exchange, possessions and instrumentally oriented organizations.
Dynamically developing system.
Initiative in defining new goals.
Conjugal family the unit of mobility.
Open class system -- individual rewards and life styles.

II. L PHASE

(UNIVERSALISTIC - QUALITY SOCIETY)
EXAMPLE: PRE WWI GERMANY

Classificatory emphasis.
Achievements are means to collective ends.
Emphasis on status and titles.
Collectivism.
Tendency to diffuseness.
Esteem vs approval.
Strong inhibitions of affectivity (emotion).
Tendency to aggression.
Tendency to political influence.
Strong emphasis on the State.

III. G PHASE

(PARTICULARISTIC-PERFORMANCE)
EXAMPLE: CLASSICAL CHINA AND MEDIEVAL SOCIETY

Value objects for what they <u>do</u>.
Criteria is relational to a situation.
Passive.
"Proper" pattern of adaption.
Collective responsibility.

Subordinate instrumental and spontaneous expression.
Superiority over competence.
Authoritarian.
Unequivocal acceptance of kinship ties.
Spontaneous affectivity strongly inhibited.
Favors "moralistic" attitude of responsibility to the unit.
Non-instrumental.
Traditionalistic.

IV. I PHASE
(PARTICULARISTIC-QUALITY)
EXAMPLE: EARLY SPANISH AMERICAN
Relational --around kinship and local community.
Society and community seen as "given" and passively "adapted to".
Work - a necessary evil.
Expressive.
Traditionalistic.
Stable.
Individualistic.
Non-,or anti-authoritarian.
Lack of concern with the structure of society.
Indifference to larger social issues.
Susceptible to "dictatorship".

Source: THE SOCIAL SYSTEM, pp. 182 ff.

The situation where the qualities of the predominating phase have a preponderant influence on all the other phases is called "Spilldown" (See Figure 15). The Goal Attainment Phase as a system goal commitment is a special case of spilldown. Thus in the United States, the General Theory of Action sees the influence of the A Phase system throughout the total System of Action. In some cases this can be dysfunctional if the functional objectives of the phase are inhibited by the presence of the spilldown.

SPILLDOWN

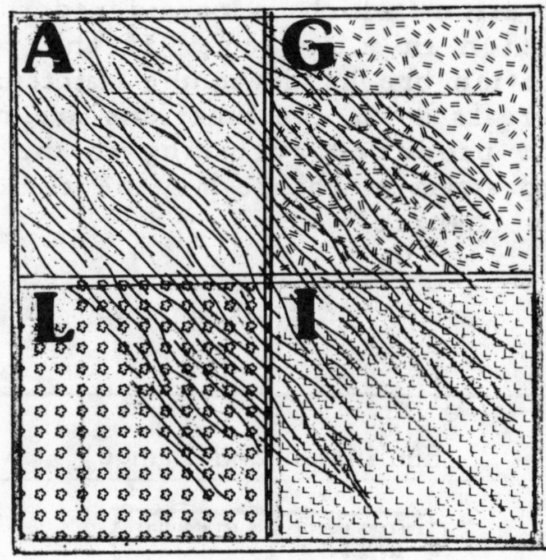

FIGURE 15

VI. FUNCTION AND ENVIRONMENT

Returning to the concepts of function and environment, it is now possible to add another dimension to the System of Action as a theoretical device. **Any** designated system has as its environment the system which is on its boundary -- which interfaces with it (See Plate VII). The boundary of the phase identified as level #1, the G Phase, is the level #1 A Phase and the level #1 I Phase. The boundary of the phase identified as level #2, the G Phase of the L Phase, is the level #1 A Phase, the level #1 I Phase, the level #2 I Phase and the level #2 A Phase. The boundaries of the level #3 G Phase, are the level #2 A Phase, the level #2 I phase, the level #3 A phase, and the level #3 I Phase. The boundary is always that system which **interfaces** the system in question.

Recall that a function is an output or message sent and received over systems. It is a relationship between theoretical systems. Every system is in many relationships with boundary systems, and this is indicated by the arrows in Plate VII. These boundary relationships are called "Boundary Maintenance" or "Interpenetration" which is considered the locus of communication in a system. If the functional interpenetration breaks down, the maintenance of the boundaries breaks down, the functions are not carried out, or not produced according to the prescribed qualities, and strain or change may be the result (see Figure 16 on Change).

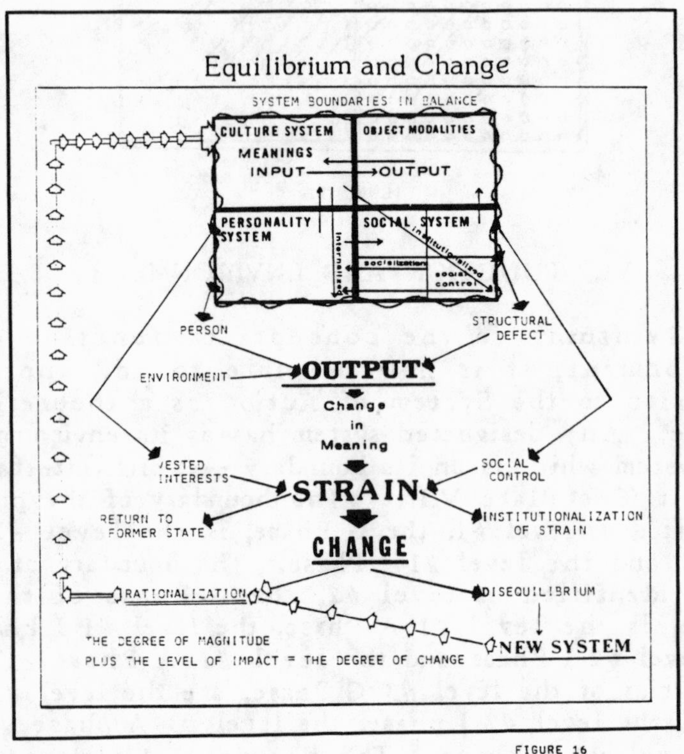

FIGURE 16

VII. EQUILIBRIUM

A state of equilibrium refers to a situation where the boundary maintenance is held, and most simply, the system of relationships is able to survive in its environment. Sometimes the "survival" varies in degree so that a state of equilibrium can be more or less stable. This means that boundary interchanges are smooth, rough, or weak. Nevertheless, no matter what the degree or type of interchange, by means of these relationships the system is able to continue **as a system** in its environment.

This can be likened to a chemical equilibrium. Two chemicals are placed in a beaker. Instead of engaging in a process which results in a new substance, these chemicals simply go back and forth from one state to another. They do not explode; they do not die out. They just never reach any resolution of the process. The state of activity continues, contained in the beaker. This view of equilibrium differs from the balance system where two weights are placed in pans held at a common mid-point. The two pans move up and down until they finally stop, and this is called their state of equilibrium. This is a static perception of equilibrium, and the chemical mode is a dynamic one.

The General Theory of Action uses the dynamic conception of equilibrium similar to the chemical one. The premise is that activity and relationships continue within given bounds. There is constant functional interchange at the system boundaries throughout the System of Action. The System of Action maintains itself in an environment and does not have any major structural alteration in the process.

VIII. CONCLUSION

The System of Action is a major device for theoretical analysis. By comparing the expected qualities of a phase with what is found by observation,

Social and Cultural Systems can be evaluated. This method also provides means for offering suggested systems of behavior to deal with problems that occur in real situations. However, this type of analysis lacks the precision which is supplied by the Pattern Variables.

6

THE PATTERN VARIABLES

A Pattern Variable is a **dichotomy of categories used to classify the choices made by an actor in determining the meaning of a situation.** Pattern Variables do not represent choices, but **categories** used to identify and separate choices. There are six Pattern Variable sets, each with two opposite classifications, making 12 Pattern Variables.

The Pattern Variables are intrinsic to the Functional Imperatives of the System of Action. In fact, they are a means of systematizing the qualitative requirements of each Phase in order to provide clear categories to be used in comparison and contrast. Each Quality of the four Phases is characterized by a Pattern Variable set of four of the twelve Pattern Variables. These are paired to emphasize orientations called Performance Norms and Sanction Norms. (See Plate IX).

The Pattern Variables are a major instrument used to create the extreme flexibility in the General Theory of Action. Much as numbers are extremely simple, but complex in their application, so the Pattern Variables are simple, yet permit complex applications on a level similar to that of mathematics.

The dichotomous trait of the Pattern Variables is theoretical in nature. There is no intention to indicate that real actors's choices are dichotomous. They are not. The categories of the Pattern Variables are dichotomous because they are **systems to classify** choices. Given typical choices made by typical actor-systems, the Pattern Variables are cells that these choices can be placed in to analyze them. The cell is not the choice. It is just a category to separate types of choices.

The Pattern Variables are somewhat like algebra in that they are not dependent on content. In algebra the figures do not specify any given set of numbers. So that a + b = c can refer to 1 + 2 = 3 or 10 + 20 = 30. The same is true of statistics or the formulas of physics. The categories are not dependent on some specific value. If speed is being measured, it can be the speed of a car, a man, a bird or light. In a Pattern Variable, the category of Universalism can be used to refer to standards for cars, typing, term papers, dog shows, sail boat races, etc. Furthermore, the specific standards are not critical to the category. It does not matter what standards you use, just so you are evaluating all the objects in the class according to the same standards. A typing teacher can evaluate students on the number of words they type, the number of words they type correctly, the amount of time it takes, or if they sit up straight. Also, as in statistics or physics, the values of the Pattern Variables can be positive or negative. Affectivity can refer to a positive or negative impulsive choice. Affective-Neutrality / Specificity can be thought of as approval or disapproval, etc.

The Pattern Variables are used individually, in pairs, and in sets of four, but an introduction to them needs to be done by means of each dichotomous category. Once the meaning of the Pattern Variables is clear, they can be combined in different sets to fit the Functional Imperatives.

I. PATTERN VARIABLES DEFINED

Each Pattern Variable set represents a dilemma, one side of which must be chosen by an actor in order to determine the meaning of a situation and to provide the basis for action. The sets are as follows:

AFFECTIVE/AFFECTIVE NEUTRALITY

UNIVERSALISM/PARTICULARISM

QUALITY/PERFORMANCE

SPECIFICITY/DIFFUSENESS

INTERNAL/EXTERNAL

INSTRUMENTAL/CONSUMMATORY

The Pattern Variables can be thought of as two different modes of orientation: those where they apply to the orientation of an actor system, and where the focus is upon the object. This reflects the earlier distinction made between actor-ego and object shown on Plate II.

ACTOR RESPONSE

Affective/Affective Neutrality
Internal/External

FOCUS ON OBJECTS

Universalism/Particularism
Quality/Performance
Specificity/Diffuseness
Instrumental/Consummatory

A. AFFECTIVE/AFFECTIVE NEUTRALITY

Affective: impulse
Affective Neutrality: discipline

The dilemma of gratification of impluse versus discipline. When confronted with situations in which particular impulses press for gratification, an actor faces the problem of whether the impulses should be spontaneously released or restrained. He can solve the problem by giving primacy to immediate gratification, or he can restrain his desire for gratification.

You are very angry. The response to anger can be placed into two categories - spontaneous release of impluse or discipline (though the response of a real person in a real event is not found in such simple opposites). The impulsive response is to spontaneously give vent to the anger by shouting, yelling, and venting the strong emotions felt. The other category is that of control. The person can stay still, not say anything, and otherwise keep their temper in check. In the first case of giving primacy to immediate gratification of the impluse is an example of categorizing according to Affectivity. The second case of exercising discipline over the impulse is an example of categorizing according to Affective Neutrality.

B. UNIVERSALISM/PARTICULARISM

Universalistic: transcendence
Particularistic: immanence

The dilemma of transcendence verses immanence. In confronting any situation, the actor faces the dilemma whether to treat the objects in the situation in accordance with a general norm covering **all** objects in that class, or whether to treat the objects in accordance with norms related to their standing in some particular relationship to him or his collectivity, independently of the objects' subsumibility under a general norm. (It is important to remember that this Pattern Variable set refers to kinds of **norms** to be used in evaluating an object).

A policeman sees a car doing 80 miles an hour in a school zone. He stops the car and finds out the driver is his wife. The policeman's response to this situation can also be placed into two dichotomous categories. One would see his choice as using the norms that apply to all objects in the class of actors who break the speed limits in school zones and give her a ticket, or to give primacy to the standards that have developed in their special relationship as husband and wife, and use those unique standards in making the decision of whether or not to give her the ticket.

In this set of categories, the words **my** or **your** indicate a unique relationship that has special norms that exist between the actor and the object. People have only **one** wife (supposedly), and she is "**my** wife." People have only one mother who is "**my** mother." A person does not treat all "mothers" as though they were their own mother. Between a person's spouse or mother there exists a unique set of relationships and norms, so they would not be treated as strangers or acquaintances. This relationship does not have to be a positive one. The policeman could stop his ex-wife, and on the basis of a bad relationship, be extremely harsh, citing her for every infraction in the book.

Another example of the dilemma represented by the categories of Particularism and Universalism often occurred in John Wayne movies. The cowboy-hero, John Wayne is injured and near death. The villain finds him, takes him to his cabin, cares for him, and saves his life. This situation now places this alter in two categories for the hero: one, that of villain who should be treated as all villains who rob, kill, and harass actors. Or, a villain who has saved his life. To the hero, he becomes one who "saved my life." This villain is now different and subject to unique rules, and that is because a new, unique relationship has come about as an event. John Wayne and the villain part. One day John Wayne comes upon a bank robbery, and finds this villain who saved his life to be the bank robber. Should he shoot him down, or make a special exception. John Wayne usually lets him go, (Particularism) and says, "now we're even" meaning next time Universalistic norms will prevail.

The basis for the unique norms seen in the relationships of Particularism can also be found in common membership in a collectivity. Members may or may not know each other. For example, a man lives in New York City and owns a small grocery store. His policy is to take cash only. He was born and brought up on a Kibbutz in Israel. One day a woman comes into his store with no money. She has just moved into the neighborhood and needs some credit. In the conversation he finds she recently arrived in New York from Israel and had been a member of the same Kibbutz where he was born. He may choose to recognize the common ties and the unique standards that are associated with their common background in making the decision about giving her credit rather than treat her in the same class as all customers who come to his store, none of whom get credit for any reason.

Changing from one class to another does not indicate a shift to a Particularistic category. If the boss is hiring a new secretary and he gets 10 who meet the typing standards, and now decides a blonde will be the next category, the choice is not defined as Particularistic. He has just changed the class of objects and the general norms that relate to that class.

In the case of Universalism, class means a category, and is relative to the definition of the actor. It can change depending on the definition of the situation by the actor. If the actor has to choose a new secretary, the class becomes "applicants for the secretarial job." If the actor has to direct traffic, the class becomes "all actors in the traffic flow." The supposition is that the actor has a set of norms or standards that apply to all objects in that class, and those standards are used equally for all the objects. Objects can also be those defined by the actor as physical or cultural, as well as social.

C. QUALITY/PERFORMANCE

Quality: what an object is
Performance: what an object does

The dilemma of object modalities. When confronting an object in a situation, the actor faces the dilemma of deciding how to treat it. Is he to treat it in the light of what it is in itself or in the light of what it does or what might flow from its actions. (At one time Parsons called these Pattern Variables Ascription and Achievement).

Quality/Performance is a matter of perspective. It is not a characteristic of an object, but a point of view taken by the actor about an object. An object does not "possess" the elements of the distinction between what it **is** and **does.**

You meet Justice Sandra Day O'Connor, the first woman to serve on the Supreme Court of the United States. You can look at her as a woman who is a Justice of the Supreme Court, with the emphasis on the fact that she is a woman (Quality), or you can examine the kinds of decisions she has made and the consequences of those decisions, which would be categorized as a focus on Performance.

You want to buy a new car. You can go to the showroom and ask the salesman about the performance characteristics of the car, such as its speed, gasoline consumption, cornering ability, safety record in crash tests, etc.(Performance). Or, you can buy the car because it is a Corvette, Rolls Royce, or a Cadilliac (Quality).

D. SPECIFICITY/DIFFUSENESS

Specificity: prior limit
Diffuseness: no prior limit

The dilemma of the scope of significance of the object. In confronting an object, an actor must choose among the various possible ranges in which he will respond to the object. The dilemma consists in whether he should respond to many aspects of the object, or to a restricted range of them previously established.

With this Pattern Variable it helps to remember that the focus is not on the actor, but on the object. It is **not** a means of describing the **degree of response** of an actor. It is the designation of the scope of modalities of an **object** that will have salience in a situation and if a decision has been made before hand to limit the range of modalities that could be the focus of attention of the actor. In the Diffuse category, there is no prior limit on the type or number of aspects of an object which **could** become the focus of attention in a situation. In the Specificity category, there is a **prior limit** on the type and number of aspects of an object which can become the focus of attention in a situation.

Diffuseness does not mean that the actor pays attention to **all** aspects of an object in a situation. In fact, a very limited range may be involved in a given situation. The point of this Pattern Variable is that there is a **prior limit set on the extent** of aspects of an object that will be admissible in a situation.

A doctor's orientation to patients can thus be segregated into two opposite categories. Before someone goes to a doctor, there is an assumed limit set on the aspects of the patient that the doctor will pay attention to. The doctor will limit his concern to your health matters, and does not ask you to join his political party or want you to listen to his personal troubles. In fact, some doctors are very specialized, so an eye, ear, nose, throat doctor will not look at hip difficulties, entertain heart problems, or fix teeth (Specificity). On the other hand, mothers will probably consider any problem that relates to their children, for mothers usually do not set a prior limit on the aspects of the object, their child. The response of psychiatrists or ministers to patients or suppliants also can be looked at as fitting into the category that stresses an openness to any aspect of a social object that comes up (Diffuseness).

Or think of a chair. Most of the time it is seen as having a limited function -- it is a place to sit.

However a child has no preset ideas about what chairs are for and thus can see it as almost anything -- a castle, a horse, a bridge, a friend, a gun, a ship, a tree, etc. There is no prior limit on the features of the chair that could become important in the situation (Diffuse). For the adult, however, there is a prior limit on the traits of the chair (Specific). Commedians and artists often tend to see objects without prior limits and that is what makes their insights so delightful.

E. INTERNAL/EXTERNAL ORIENTATION

Internal: private interests
External: collective interests

The dilemma of private versus collective interests, or the distribution between private permissiveness and collective obligation. (At one time Parsons called these Pattern Variables Self-Orientation and Collective orientation).

The quarterback of a small, winning college football team is their star, and there is no question that the team's success comes from his performance on the field. The team has made the playoff game for the national championship in the league. Everyone would get to fly to Hawaii and the school would get a financial bonus if the team won. However, the student who is the quarterback has always wanted to go to Harvard Law School. However he needs a scholarship, and has been working for years to realize his dream. A letter comes from Harvard stating that he must be present at Harvard for the final scholarship interview on the date of the playoff game. Harvard will not change the date. He will have to forfeit the scholarship if he is absent, and he is assured that he will probably get the scholarship if he is there for the interview. The team is also sure to lose if he doesn't play. They are almost sure to win if he does play. This dilemma can be thought about in terms of two Pattern Variable categories: one, does the quarterback give primacy to his private interests and go to Harvard for the interview (Internal), or does he give primacy to the collective interests and play for the team (External).

F. INSTRUMENTAL/CONSUMMATORY

Instrumental: object as a means to an end
Consummatory: object as an end

The dilemma of whether to treat an object as an end in itself, or as a means to an end.

There are two friends who work together. One is kind, trusting, and is quite bright about the work that has to be done. The relationship of one friend to the other can be examined on the basis of two opposite perspectives that see the friend in two different modes. One, does the actor look at his friend simply as a friend (Consummatory), or does he look at the friend as someone who can be a means of his own advancement in the company (Instrumental). Another illustration can be used to classify the way actors think about stamp collections. In one case actors can be seen as enjoying stamps for themselves, their beauty, the skill involved in making them, etc. (Consummatory), or actors can be seen as looking at the stamps as a means to make money (Instrumental).

II. THE PATTERN VARIABLE COMBINATIONS

Only the first four of these Pattern Variable sets are used in relation to the Functional Imperatives. The last two are considered a constant choice, and are implicit in each situation. Here, we will concentrate on the four Pattern Variables related to the Qualities related to the four Functional Imperatives. Please turn to Plate VIII.

A. AFFECTIVE/AFFECTIVE NEUTRALITY AND SPECIFICITY/DIFFUSENESS

This set of two Pattern Variables can be understood best as a four cell matrix and each set can be seen in its positive mode, as it is in the matrix, or in its negative mode.

1. Segmental Gratification:

This orientation involves finding a receptive and/or responsive object and finding a response from that object only in a context of direct, immediate gratification, and without any regard for responsibilities beyond it.

An example of this Pattern Variable combination can be seen in the relationship involved in prostitution. The action is sought in order to gratify an impluse, and there is no further involvement beyond the specific encounter. There are no ties, no commitments, and no responsibilities. There is a prior limit on the modalities of the object that are to be involved in the relationship (Specificity), and the object is to gratify an immediate impulse (Affectivity).

Another example could be the swearing you do when you hit your finger with a hammer. There is some satisfaction in letting off steam, but you probably do not really literally "mean" what you say and certainly don't intend to carry out the epithets.

2. Approval:

This orientation involves approval or disapproval of an object with respect to value standards governing specific types of modalities without regard to responsibilities outside the specific context. Approval is a non-emotional means of demonstrating an evaluative response to an object on the basis of a restricted set of modalities that have been limited prior to the evaluation.

In this case, a manager may approve the typing skill of a secretary. There is a standard in the office, and secretaries are evaluated according to it with no emotional input, and with no ramifications beyond what is involved in the job. A sales division may list the sales of each salesperson in the department with a line dividing those who have met and exceeded their quota, and those who sold less than their quota. In another illustration, a company may be looking for a piece of metal that can be twisted a lot without breaking for a new kind of toy. That is the only modality of the metal they are concerned with (not who makes it, where it comes from, or even how much it costs) (Specificity), and they are completely unemotional in the process of approving the performance of the metal (Affective/Neutrality).

3. Love:

This is an orientation where there is an emotional, unrestrained reaction to an object in its entirety, and without regard to any particular content, specific gratification, or specific qualifications.

When a parent loves a child, there is no qualification which stipulates that the love is only in effect if the child is good, or gets "A"s in school. When an art object, or car, is "loved," there is an unrestrained emotional response (Affective) coupled with no prior limits set on the aspects of the object that are to be the focus of this emotion (Diffuseness).

4. Esteem:

In this orientation, there is no prior limit set on the aspects of the object, and no particular context of specific modalities under consideration, but the evaluation is made in an unemotional, disciplined way.

Usually actors look upon those in medical and teaching professions with esteem. There is respect, and it extends to all aspects of the actor or object. Thus it is assumed that doctors and teachers will be deserving of respect in all aspects of their lives, even though the original evaluation is made on the basis of occupational skills and achievements (Diffuseness). This is not a highly emotional response however (Affective Neutrality).

Each of these orientations can be found in its opposite case, thus there can be segmental dissatisfaction; disapproval; hate; and disrespect.

B. UNIVERSALISM/PARTICULARISM AND QUALITY/PERFORMANCE

This Pattern Variable matrix also includes a combination of four Pattern Variables and their "translation."

<u>1. Conformity with universal norms</u>:

This orientation involves conformity with a universalistic standard governing objects possessing certain qualities universalistically assessed.

Men are expected to be strong. The class here is men, and the Quality, or what the object "is," is strength. Ministers are expected to be sensitive. Rocks are expected to be hard. In each of these examples, we evaluate the objects as part of a category to which the same norms apply(Universalism), and the object is looked at in terms of what it "is" (Quality), not what it "does."

2. Orientation by virtue of particular prior relationship:

Here the orientation involves conformity with a standard governing the conduct of objects possessing certain qualities assessed in the light of their particular relationship to the actor.

In this case, an actor may expect objects to meet certain general standards because of the unique relationship involved. Thus, actors may trust a friend because he is **their** friend. They would not be so inclined just because he is "someone's" friend. This can also apply to objects such as cars, because it is seen as "my" car, or the radio controlled plane that is "mine," and that "I built." It is better because it is "mine." Actors often have a unique set of expectations or norms that apply to their mothers, fathers, and children, **because** it is "their" mother, father, or child.

3. Successful accomplishment:

This orientation involves an expectation of achievement in accordance with a universalistic standard of attainment of a minimum level of satisfactory performance or a requisite degree of excellence above that minimum.

Taking a driving license test is one example of successful accomplishment. There is a minimum standard required for the written test as well as the actual driving test. If these standards are met, the license is granted. In sports, the actor must meet a minimum standard to make the team, however, if a team or athlete breaks a standing record for performance, as in the high jump, there is an example of successful accomplishment that involves a degree of excellence beyond the minimum. This can also apply to objects that must meet certain criteria of strength, flexibility, etc. before being approved for sale. The same standards apply to all objects being evaluated, (Universalism), and the expectation involves a performance (Performance).

<u>4. Obligations of particular relationship or membership:</u>

An orientation of action where the expectation of performance is in conformity with a standard of achievement appropriate to a particular membership in a class or relationship independent of universalistically defined standards of performance.

Congressmen, teachers, and any public or private official can get into grave trouble if they permit themselves to be bribed. A bribery is an action which requires a type of special performance norms distinct from other actors in the class. The contractor will be given special consideration for the public building project, the teacher will change a grade, the official will overlook certain permit requirements, etc. Because of the particular relationship between relatives, they are often not permitted to serve in positions that would place them in a position to do favors for family members because it is generally recognized that such ties place family members outside the universal standards for performance. There is pressure for favoritism. The mayor may ignore certain performance requirements for his brother to be hired into the accounting office, etc. The brother would expect the mayor to do this **because** he is his brother. These expectations focus upon Performance, and the standards are Particularistic, i.e., norms unique to the relationship between the actor and the objects.

Each of these sets of four Pattern Variables is distinguished from each other by its general focus. The first set involving Affectivity/Affective Neutrality and Specificity/Diffuseness are seen as "Sanction Norms" or ways of evaluating an object. The second set including Universalism/Particularism and Quality/Performance are considered "Performance Norms" which are primarily related to role expectations.

These two sets of four Pattern Variables each are not the only combinations possible. In fact, Parsons developed many more, but these two sets are the ones he primarily used in the General Theory of Action, and thus will be the only combinations discussed here.

III. CULTURE SYSTEM, SOCIAL SYSTEM, AND PERSONALITY SYSTEM LEVELS

Each Pattern Variable, and each of the above Pattern Variable sets can be used with each of the sub-systems of the General Theory of Action. The Culture System level frames the Pattern Variable as a set of **meaning patterns**; the Social System level as a pattern of **role expectations**; and the Personality System as a pattern of **need dispositions.**

To use the Pattern Variables on these levels, the term meaning system, role expectation or need disposition is put before the definition of the Pattern Variable. Thus Affectivity can be a meaning system (Culture System), a role expectation (Social System), or a need disposition (Personality System) where primacy is given to immediate gratification of an impulse. The **meaning** (Culture System) of tears is the unrestrained manifestation of sorrow; the **role expectation** (Social System) is that the relatives of someone who has died are expected to cry; and some actors have a **need disposition** (Personality System) to cry when they are in a sorrowful situation, even if those involved are strangers.

Using Affective Neutrality, the meaning of no tears on the part of the minister represents strength

(Culture System); men are not expected to cry in most situations (Social System); and some actors have a need disposition never to exhibit any emotion (Personality System).

This procedure can be carried out for all the Pattern Variables, and the combination sets of the Pattern Variables.

IV. PATTERN VARIABLES AND THE SYSTEM OF ACTION

With this chapter, the presentation of all of the segments of the General Theory of Action is completed. The fusion of the Pattern Variables into the framework of the System of Action and its sub-systems with the underlying grid of the Functional Imperatives rounds off the basic working device of the General Theory of Action.

Plate IX fits the Pattern Variables into the four Phases of the System of Action together with the Qualities of each Phase. This set shows what the Pattern Variables, Qualities, and Sanction Norms should be associated with each Functional Imperative. It is the standard to be used for comparison while using the General Theory of Action.

Each set of Pattern Variables is identified as related to Performance Norms (P.N.) or Sanction Norms (S.N.). However, Pattern Variables do not always need to be thought of in these sets. While doing an analysis, single Pattern Variables can be identified, as well as combinations that cross the sets (for example, Universalism-Affective Neutrality). This basic blocking of the Pattern Variables into the four Phases is the same for any level of the System of Action or its sub-systems of Culture System, Social System, and Personality System. The Elements of Action constitute the fundamental assumption, and of Action constitute the fundamental assumption, and the actor becomes the focus or point of reference. However the means of analysis is through the Pattern Variables and the four Phases of the System of Action, and not the categories established as Elements of Action.

A. ADAPTIVE PHASE

In the Adaptive Phase, the Quality is Technical Competence. The Performance Norm is technical efficiency, and the Pattern Variables associated with technical efficiency are the Universalism-Performance set, which translates into successful accomplishment. The Sanction Norm is approval/disapproval, and the associated Pattern Variables are Specificity-Affective Neutrality, which translates as approval. The Functional Imperative is survival in an environment. On this level there is a focus upon the manipulation of objects.

B. LATENT PATTERN MAINTENANCE PHASE

The Quality of the Latent Pattern Maintenance Phase is Cultural Value Commitment. The Performance Norm is cultural responsibility with the associated Pattern Variables of Quality-Universalism which translate as conformity to universal norms. The Sanction Norm is showing esteem and those associated Pattern Variables are affective Neutrality-Diffuseness, which translate as esteem. The Functional Imperative is socialization and tension control. This Phase is oriented toward the maintenance of the institutionalization of the value system.

C. INTEGRATIVE

The Quality of the Integrative Phase is loyalty. The Performance Norm is showing solidarity, and the associated Pattern Variable set is Particularism-Quality, which is translated as prior relationship to actor-ego. The Sanction Norm is diffuse acceptance, and the Pattern Variable set is Diffuseness-Affectivity, which translates as love. The Functional Imperative is social control.

D. GOAL ATTAINMENT

The Quality of the Goal Attainment Phase falls into two divisions: a)system goal commitment (when the whole system of action is emphasizing the G Phase), and b) legitimation of unit-goal commitment (when some other Phase is emphasized). In the case of a) the Performance Norm is system or "relational" responsibility, and in b) the Performance Norm is requisite rules of the game. For both, the Pattern Variable set is Performance-Particularism which translates as prior relationship to a class. The Sanction Norm for both is conditional response reward, and the Pattern Variable set is Affectivity-Specificity which translates as segmental gratification. The Functional Imperative is the mobilizing of the necessary prerequisites for attainment of system goals. Here the system maximizes favorable or gratifying conditions for system goal attainment.

The Pattern Variables are one of the important keys for analysis with the General Theory of Action. In one way, they resemble the simplicity of mathematics. There are only ten numbers, and each is simple in itself. These numbers are combined subject to varying levels of sophistication in the rules, and the complexity of mathematics evolves. The Pattern Variables are also each simple and are limited to six sets or twelve categories. The System of Action and all its sub-systems prescribe the rules of application, and from this emerges the intricacy of analysis of the General Theory of Action. Each of the parts of the General Theory of Action is simple. The intricacy comes about in the combinations that are possible among all of these parts.

7

USING THE GENERAL THEORY OF ACTION

Basically, the use of the General Theory of Action involves the processes of comparison and contrast. The Functional Imperatives coupled with the Pattern Variables and the System of Action indicate what one would expect to find in a successful system, regardless of the content of the values or the details of behavior systems. The General Theory of Action is then used to analyze actual systems to compare them to the expected configuration. The analysis should identify divergencies, anomalies, contradictions, and points of tension, while at the same time indicating directions that could be taken to rectify these problems. The General Theory of Action also provides a means of tracing the communication systems of organizations and their effectiveness. It is a template for the analysis of change over time, and a guide for assessing the consistency of systems with each other.

It should be made clear that the General Theory of Action does not assume that a state of equilibrium of a given system is to be desired. The point is that if any system, evil or good, is to continue to survive in its environments, it will require a certain degree of system cohesiveness or the strain will overwhelm it, destroying it, or changing it radically (See Figure 16). The General Theory of Action can be used to analyze Hitler's Germany, or the structure of the local bicycle shop. The process of study does not necessarily condone what is being examined.

The best example of this application of this procedure can be found in the work of Professor Parsons himself. Most of his essays have, as their underlying framework, an initial analysis done with the General Theory of Action, and it is hoped that you will read one or two of them to see this for yourself.

Frequently it was Parsons' practice not to stress the terminology of the General Theory of Action, but rather to translate this analysis into the general language of the intellectual community.

Some brief examples of this "translation" process will be given, to show you how the theory is used, but it is important to remember that ideas taken out of context lose a lot of their impact. They really only make sense as part of a total argument which is to be found in reading the complete Parsonian essays and attempting to discern the basic theory. Please follow along with Plate IX.

I. SAMPLES FROM SOME OF PROFESSOR PARSONS ESSAYS

In 1964 Professor Parsons gave a lecture at the University of California, at Los Angeles entitled, "Death and American Society."[10] His thesis was that the American attitude toward death is traceable to the prevalence of Adaptive Phase orientations which pervade American society. Some of the arguments he uses to make that point follow:

Regarding death, he said that "the **modern attitude**," conspicuous in the United States, is one of **bringing to bear every possible resource to prolong life.**" [Emphasis not in the original. It is used here to highlight the segments reflecting the theory.] The Adaptive Phase represents a concern with survival in the environment by means of technical competence. The Pattern Variables of this Phase are the elements of technical competence, and so modern medicine shows a commitment to survival by means of technical competence. We do everything technically possible to prolong life.

He goes on to point out that Americans "do not like to accept the fact of death unless it is felt to be inevitable, i.e. **from causes essentially beyond human control.**" With an Adaptive Phase orientation, death that is beyond the scope of technical competence of the day is more acceptable, such as the death of those who are very old or who have what is thought to be an incurable disease. However, those who die from accidents or anything that could be considered man-made, as a seat belt not being used, or someone forgetting to take the door off of an abandoned refigerator, represent a great tragedy because there was a lack of technical competence. Someone could have done something to prevent such a death. Parsons continues this point by saying that "the fact of premature death,...in terms of the 'modern temper' very often cannot be treated as anything but **man-made** in some sense, whether it be by what in **any conceivable sense is controllable or preventable** disease, by accident, crime or war."

"A **certain realism in facing the facts** of the world is characteristic of the scientific attitude." Here there is a complete translation of both sets of Pattern Variables associated with the Adaptive Phase: Universalism/Performance, Specificity/Affective Neutrality. Realism is associated with a lack of emotion, an impartial evaluation of what happens under conditions that are to be as objective as is possible, repeatable, and with a strict focus on the experimental details.

"The meaning of the life of the individual unit -- and hence its termination -- derives from **the place occupied by that unit in a larger and more comprehensive system** which is a structure but even more is involved in temporal process far transcending the life-space of the individual." In the Adaptive Phase American Society, "the task of the individual is to **maximize his responsible and competent contribution** to the general **task,** to have lived a maximally 'worth while' life in the **doing of important things.**" Such emphasis places the individual as the unit of approval or disapproval in the occupational sphere, in life tasks, and to evaluate the value of a life as lived. If an American is asked who he/she is, the reply is usually in terms of occupaton: a pilot, a housewife, a dentist, a bookeeper, a salesman, etc. This is generally the unit of evaluation also, as reflected in the facilities and rewards. The dentist may make more money than the bookeeper, and this is considered a rewarding life. Some women feel the role of housewife is not meaningful enough and they opt to seek careers or success in the occupational field. The pilot who quits to live in a hippie commune is often considered an unfortunate failure, even though he may have achieved great personal inner peace of mind. Thus, the individual in an Adaptive Phase system is very much alone; "The most acceptable death is that which comes at the end of a full life in which the individual can be said to come somewhere near having maximized the opportunities given him by his capacities and his situation, and having chosen worth-while goals, has either **achieved** them, or if he has failed, has done so through **no fault of his own.**" All of these points are derived from the logic of the Adaptive Phase system as the emphasized Phase, along with the set of four Pattern Variables that accompany it.

Given this line of thinking, he goes on to say that "there seems to be no doubt of the genuineness of the predominant deep repugnance to most Americans to involvement in war." (Since the meaning of life is to be successful by showing technical competence, war deprives young men of this opportunity and thus goes against a fundamental value of the Adaptive Phase American society.) "Furthermore, of course, war is conceived to be **intrinsically preventable** (subject to human control or Adaptive Phase orientations which can prevent death), and thus unacceptable if not prevented where possible."

However, there is an alternative to this. When the whole society shifts emphasis from the Adaptive Phase to the Goal Attainment Phase with system goal commitment, the situation is changed. Parsons says: "If, however, there are circumstances in which war seems to be forced upon a nation then its acceptance is in certain respects a supreme test of **collective responsibility....**In these circumstances (WW II), for the individual to risk his life in a war is very clearly considered in a context of national loyalty to be the supreme sacrifice....It can be said that war on a grand scale in which national security is genuinely at stake (where the whole system does not convert to emphasize the Goal Attainment Phase) is something very difficult for us to accept....Clearly death in war belongs in the category of the adventitious occasions (which can be prevented)....Furthermore, of course war is conceived to be **intrinsically preventable** (Adaptive Phase orientation) and, above all a fundamental evil....Nationally we are extremely sensitive to the **line** between taking risks in international affairs 'short of war,' and the transition to the status of a 'shooting war'" (war with the Adaptive Phase predominate or war where there is a complete transition to the Goal Attainment Phase). During this lecture, given in 1964, Professor Parsons commented that the U.S. would have difficulties carrying on the Vietnam war (as a war in the context of an Adaptive Phase society) -- a prediction which was to come true.

In another essay, Professor Parsons explores the transition role that Christianity played in the development of modern industrial (Adaptive Phase) social systems ("Christianity and Modern Industrial Society"11). He makes the point that "the structure of the medieval church came to serve...as a model of social organization which could be extended into secular society....It made possible a social island that **institutionalized a universalistic basis of role-allocation manifested in careers open to talent** (the Pattern Variable of Universalism, coupled with Performance, evaluated in an Affectively Neutral-Specificity mode)....The Christian church developed for its own internal use a highly **rationalized and codified** body of norms which underlay the legal structure of the whole subsequent development of Western society." (Again, rational and codified translate as the Adaptive Phase emphasis of Affective Neutrality, Universalism, and Specificity.) Calvinistic doctrine produced a "powerful impetus to the acceptance of **individual responsibility.**"

In schools the mode of emphasis shifted. The teacher now had a new primary function: "to help equip the child for a responsible role in society when his education has been completed" (the Latent Pattern Maintenance orientation). To a much higher degree the question of how far he takes advantage of this opportunity becomes his own responsibility" (Adaptive Phase).

This Christian emphasis on individualism came to hold that "any acceptance of life in this world as of value entails **acceptance of the value of the means necessary to do approved things effectively**" (Adaptive Phase Pattern Variables). A concomitant theme of Christianity was "a certain strain toward equalitarianism, associated with the conception of the dignity of the individual human being." Responsibilty of the individual came to be seen as first, the "responsibility **of** the individual in that he cannot rely on a dependent relation to others, or to some authority, to absolve him of responsibility -- this is the aspect we have been referring to as **autonomy....**The other aspect is responsibility **for** and **to**, responsibility for **results** and to other persons and to collectivities." (Responsibility is another translation for the Pattern Variables of the Adaptive Phase which emphasizes Performance, Universalism, Affective Neutrality, and Specificity).

In Parsons' article on "Democracy and Social Structure in Pre-Nazi Germany"[12] there is a good example of an analysis of a social system with a Latent Pattern Maintenance emphasis. Briefly, such a system, which stresses esteem, will also stress "titles," and the importance of the accumulation of many titles. Not to use all the relevant titles is a mark of supreme disrespect. Parsons found a "pattern of masculine superiority and a tendency to assume authority and prerogative on the part of husbands and fathers" (a characteristic of a Universalistic/Quality, Neutrality/Diffuseness orientation). In marriage, primary emphasis is placed on the man's formal status (Latent Pattern Maintenance emphasis on Universalism-Quality), whereas in the U.S. it is marriage to a particular man as an individual. Many of these persistent orientations made transition in Germany at that time to democracy (which is biased toward an Adaptive Phase system) difficult.

Again, it cannot be stressed enough that there is a real need to look at Parsons' original essays, and to read one at least entirely, in order to see how he uses the basics of the theory as the backbone of his analsyses.

II. APPLYING THE GENERAL THEORY OF ACTION

Actually, there are no set rules for applying the General Theory of Action. It is somewhat similar to problems of measurement. There are many tools to measure with, such a a ruler, a scale, and a calibrated container, along with standards using inches, pounds, gallons, miles, meters, yards, etc. You do not need every tool for every problem you encounter. You select the ones that are appropriate. So if you are measuring a book, you might use a ruler and a scale, and use the norms of inches and pounds. If you are measuring some water, you would use a measuring cup and its norms of pints and quarts. Each problem involves different standards of measurement and its own range of possible lines of approach. One crucial part of working the problem is deciding what tools and standards to use and the sequence to use them.

It might help, when using the General Theory of Action, to think of it the same way you think of the "law." In a court, the lawyer must phrase his case in terms of the relevant law. He must show how the information he has fits those laws, and conclusions are drawn only on the basis of the applied law. Facts which do not fit any legal category must be declared invalid as evidence, while at the same time the lawyer does not use all the law he knows, or is known in the world. This process is very demanding, and sometimes seems irrational to the uninformed observer. This is also the case with the application of the General Theory of Action. Information is always framed in the modes of the General Theory of Action. If there is no theoretical concept to handle the data, it is ignored. (This does not mean such data may not be important. But, to include it, a new theoretical component will have to be invented to do so -- just as Einstein's physics cannot handle the notion of anything going faster than the speed of light.) The theory is only a handle, or device to manage information.

In doing an actual analysis you may use the three Systems, the four Phases, and/or the four sets of Pattern Variables shown on Plate IX.

The following guide may be of help, however it is only a suggestion to aid you in getting started. It should not be thought of as a required set of procedures.

1. Decide what point of reference you will use. Is there an actor and object that stands out? List the actors and objects. (You will not always need to do this, but it is good to get it worked out early in your analysis).

2. Fold out Plate IX. Identify the context of the larger society of the subject you are analyzing. What predominant Phase is emphasized? What are the major qualities and Pattern Variables associated with that Phase? Since most societies emphasize one Phase over others, and since there is often spilldown from that Phase, it helps to establish the backdrop of the systems you are studying because they may have an important influence on other systems.

Sometimes the emphasized Phase can be identified by finding what the important facilities and rewards are. Thus in the United States, money is considered a more significant reward for a job well done than a change in title or praise, which can be the most significant rewards in other societies. Finding that rewards are based on occupations is a clue that points to an emphasis on the Adaptive Phase.

3. Fold out Plate V. What function are you interested in studying, and consequently, what Functional Imperative is involved, along with its Quality? What Phase, with its Pattern Variables is associated with that Functional Imperative? Another way to work this problem is to identify the roles that are important and then relate them to the Functional Imperative they are most consistent with.

4. Fold out Plate IV. What System levels are you interested in studying, Culture System, Social System, or Personality System? Often an interesting comparison can be made while looking for conflicts between what is held in a value system, how that value system is institutionalized in behavior systems, and how it has been internalized as need dispositions.

5. Sketch out the levels of systems you intend to work with, using Parsons' formats.

6. Identify the Qualities and the Pattern Variables that you would expect to find in terms of the Functional Imperatives involved in the systems you have identified. In other words, outline what you "should" find.

7. Using the Pattern Variables and/or the four Phases, generally categorize the data you have about the systems you are studying. Are they consistent with what is expected? Arrange them in a diagram form that shows what you "did" find.

8. Compare and contrast the diagrams you have developed for 5 and 6. Are they the same? Are they different? If so, where, how, and to what extent?

9. What are the implications of your findings? What could it mean? What do you see that you were not aware of before? What are the theoretical indicators

concerning conflict, resolution, change, etc. Look for contradictions on levels, between levels, in systems and between systems, and between the expected functional paradigm and what you find.

In doing this analysis, remember that Professor Parsons did not use the four Phases or the Pattern Variables inflexibly, looking at things in infinite detail. He uses them as a wide angle brush, sweeping across his field of vision. To get too involved in minutiae, especially with the Pattern Variables, tends to lead to confusion for many of those starting out with the General Theory of Action. It is better to start with more general applications and move to the intricate ones as you gain experience. In another a sense, using the General Theory of Action is also like painting. You have available a whole set of brushes, paints, and a canvas. There is no requirement that you must use all of the brushes or all of the colors. You use what suits the subject. The same is true in using Parsons' Theory. You may use some or all of the concepts available, in any order that suits the problem you are studying. A close look at some of the essays Professor Parsons wrote will help you see this.

8

APPLICATION EXERCISES

APPLICATION I
SOME SIMPLE
PATTERN VARIABLE APPLICATIONS

Identify the Pattern Variable for each of the following:

1. John gritted his teeth as the nurse walked toward him with her needle. In his pocket he had the bullet and he fully intended to bite it. Taking blood always upset him, but he wasn't going to pass out in front of anybody.

Affective or Affective Neutrality?

2. Sinking into the chair, Shep knew Jerry was coming and he owed him one this time. Jerry had put out his own money to get this rocket company going, and without him, Shep would be no where.

There are two Pattern Variables here.
Universalism or Particularism and Performance or Quality?

3. It didn't matter what his father or anyone else said. If George was going to come into this company he was going to do it just like anyone else. He would have to jump the hurdles and meet the sales standards. That was the only way.

Universalism or Particularism?

4. It was hard to believe. There he was, standing not twelve inches away--close enough to touch. How often had his picture been across the front pages of the paper, his voice on the evening news. Stephen could hardly breathe as he looked at the President of the

United States.

Quality or Performance?

5. The report was sitting on the top of the desk, but Gary couldn't see it. The tears were welling up and filling his eyes. He was seized with frustration, anger, and fear. "This Project can't fail!" he yelled as he threw it as far as he could.

Affective or Affective Neutrality?

6. Mary didn't care what Nate wanted to do or say. All she wanted to do was be with him, listen to him, watch him, do what ever he wanted. It was enough that he was finally home.

Specificity/Diffuseness?

7. Sadie was elated. The blood pulsed and her hand shook a bit as she picked up the phone. She steadied herself, drew a deep breath, and said in a deep and controlled voice, "They picked me Mom. I'll be the first woman Astronaut on the space shuttle. But I don't want them to make a big deal out of the fact I am a woman. All I want is to do my job and let that stand for itself. Some of those media people can't see an inch beyond gender."

Here the actor, Sadie, is looking at herself as the object from the point of view of the press. Turn to Plate IX, to fill in these Pattern Variable sets.

Is her reaction Affective or Affective Neutral?
What orientations does she want from the press toward her as an object?
Universalism or Particualrism?
Quality of Performance?
Specificity or Diffuseness?

8. Take each Pattern Variable set and make up your own examples. Then try to combine sets, and finally

develop a paragraph which includes the whole set of four.

9. Look at the cartoons in the daily paper to see what Pattern Variable sets you find.

APPLICATION II
"DID HIS JOB -- GOT AN "F" OFFICER SAYS"

The following article appeared in a local newspaper in the 1960's:

Do you deserve an "F" in a sensitivity course if you arrest a fellow student for possession of marijuana?

Hermosa Beach police officer William Cavanaugh says that is why he was flunked in Psychology 33 at El Camino College. An administrative board of review there began an investigation Thursday to see if he is right.

Cavanaugh and Wayne E. McDonald were students together last semester in R. Theodore Franklin's course on personality and social adjustment--a so-called sensitivity course in group communications.

Cavanaugh said that when he noticed McDonald had a one-pound brick of marijuana, he confiscated it after class and informed other officers. McDonald was later convicted of possessing marijuana and placed on two years probation.

Other members of the class got sensitive about it and voted to oust Cavanaugh. He kept attending classes even though he had one defender, student Richard Baker.

When grades were announced, both Cavanuagh and Baker got "F"s.

The two petitioned El Camino for a review of their grades and Cavanaugh, who said he needed the credit for the course to get into a four-year college, threatened to sue. He said he was an "A" student in police science.

Franklyn said through his attorney, Mary Creutz,

that Cavanaugh had an "F" coming for other reasons than the arrest.

"He didn't tell the class he was an officer when the class began," and "one of the basic parts of the course is that you be honest."

(In the 1960's, "sensitivity" usually meant that a group of people would share their feelings and thoughts as spontaneously and openly as possible. Participants were expected to feel able to discuss intimate information about themselves, such a fears, hopes, terrible secrets, tramautic experiences, etc. In many groups, occupation was not asked at the onset of the discussion to encourage people to see each other as people and not to relate to the role or occupation someone held.

There are many unanswered questions in this story, however, an interesting analysis can be done with what is provided.

In the aftermath, Franklyn resigned his position at the college at the request of the administration and both McDonald and Baker were given passing grades in the class.)

Police Officer: Cavanaugh
Arrested Student: McDonald
Teacher: Franklyn
Student who supported Cavanaugh: Baker

ANALYSIS:

1. What roles are involved in the story?

2. What Phases do these roles fit?

3. What are the Functional Imperatives and qualties of those Phases?

4. What is the relative power of the Phases to each other? Can one Phase override the other?

5. What did the role encumbants in the story "do" as part of their role?

6. Were the actions consistent with the qualities of the Phase and the Functional Imperatives involved?

7. A grade is a functional output to an environment. Was the function received by the larger system? Why?

8. What are the Pattern Variables you would expect to find in the classroom relative to the teaching process?

9. What are the Pattern Variables generaly associated with "sensitivity" groups?

10. How do these two sets of Pattern Variables differ?

11. What Pattern Variables are associated with the grading process?

12. How does the practice of letting students "vote" on whether other students can stay in the class relate to the quality associated with the "teaching" Functional Imperative?

13. How do the Pattern Variables associated with "sensitivity" groups relate to the Pattern Variables associated with grading?

14. What conclusions are suggested about the use of "sensitivity" groups in the classroom setting?

15. How do the Pattern Variables associated with law enforcement relate to those of the "sensitivity" group?

16. What can you say about the practice of having "sensitivity" groups in the classroom setting?

APPLICATION III
PHOTOGRAPHING CATS

When working with this article, it is important to remember that the photographer is the actor-ego, and the object in the situation is the cat. Focus upon the role aspect of a typical photographer and the role of a typical cat rather than thinking of a specific person or a specific cat. Use Plates VIII and IX.

Remember the following association of Pattern Variables:

ACTOR:
Affective/Affective Neutrality

ORIENTATION OF ACTOR TO OBJECT:
Universalism/Particularism
Quality/Performance
Specificity/Diffusness (The actor is NEVER "diffuse".)

When reading the article, write the relevant Pattern Variable (referred to as PV) or Phase in the right-hand margin. (A Pattern Variable can be identified by saying something is "not", thus implying its opposite.) Identify what the actor thinks should be the orientation of an actor toward cats, and what he rejects as the incorrect orientation. Don't forget that Pattern Variables can be used singly or in sets that are different from those in Plate IX (i.e. you can combine Affective Neutrality and Quality).

Remember, do not read these rigidly.

Adapted from the article, "The Hattersley Class: Stalk Your Cats". POPULAR PHOTOGRAPHY. (November) 1970.

One of the nice things about cats is that they're not people and have no desire to be. (Type of object? -- social or non-social?) They don't even desire to be cats. They should be thought of as just cats. Being psychically fufilled entities, why should you worry about what they do? (What PV is being denied here?) Each cat is a universe unto himself: beyond this, no living creature is possibly able to go.

Some people can't accept cats on this basis. They want them to be incomplete, yearning creatures like dogs. With few exceptions, people seem to want their dogs to be people instead of dogs. Since the dogs know they'll never make the grade, (what PV is implied in "make the grade"?) they do the next best thing--they try to please people. (What PV is being used by the actor to define the orientation of dogs to people? Hint: keep this in the context of "making the grade".) Naturally, people go for this because the unearned love they get from dogs supports their strange notion that they are intrinsically loveable without even trying to be and thus should get the love of other creatures by right. (What PV does "earned" and "unearned" represent? What PV would "intrinsically loveable" represent? Which ones does the actor think people should use in their orientation to creatures?)

Cats are another story. Think of them as universes unto themselves, (PV?) they are held together by love. (Phase, PV?) All universes are, for love is the great glue that holds reality together. But love on the universal level has an impartial quality (PVs for "impartial"?) that rebuffs and angers unthinking human beings. (Is this the same meaning of love in the Phase you identified?) Since it doesn't wag tails, lick your hands, buy you expensive presents, or sing you sentimental songs (What PV is represented here?) it isn't even recogonized as love. This is the impartial love of cats--not for sale (PV?), knows no favorites (PV?), never advertises, does its own thing every moment, every day. (Do not get confused here. Though the actor describes what these animals do, etc., it is the photographer's orientation to the modalities of the objects that is being shown by the description. Do not try to think of the animal as another actor relating back to the photographer.)

Bear these things in mind when you start to photograph your cat. From what I've said, you can see you shouldn't go about it as you would with your dog. If you bribe your dog with tidbits or pats on the head (PV as "should not" and its opposite, as a "should"?), he'll do anything you want that is within his understanding. If you try to bribe your cat, you'll not get what you want and you'll go against his very essence as a cat.

When we take the element of bribery (PV?) out of the photographer-model relationship, it leaves us in a unique situation, for bribery usually has a central place. We get people to pose for us and perform certain previsualized gyrations by promising them something, material or psychological in return. If they're not bribable and are ot a world entirely alien to your likes and dislikes, then what do you do? What can you do with something as entirely alien to man as a cat--a ferociously feline cat?

The answer is not to try and influence your cat at all. Let him do whatever he wants to do. (PV for "whatever he wants"?) He'll do it anyway, for that's all Mother Nature has him programmed for, and he seems to have little choice in the matter. Then borrow a page from a hunting manual and stalk him exactly the way he stalks his own prey--say, a mouse or a fly. Embark on photographing him as if you were on a hunting expedition in deepest Africa.

Now borrow another page from the manual, the one titled <u>Patience</u>. (What PVs would describe "Patience"?) As a challenge to yourself, see if you can be more patient then the cat. You will notice that for him, the process of waiting has a special quality to it. It's not an irritable shuffling or a form of slow suffering. It's a dynamic thing. Its vitality doesn't depend on expectation, but on a total awareness of and immersion in <u>now</u>. See if you can start to develop this active form of patience in yourself when you're stalking him with your camera.

Perhaps a cat's best tip to you is to learn to wait without expectation. (PV for "wait without expectation"?) That's what <u>he</u> does. Don't be waiting for specific pictures you have planned, (PV?) for that can turn waiting into a chore -- especially if they don't materialize. Try to wait because you're waiting, and for no other reason. Let waiting be a <u>now</u> thing, an experience to be savored itself.

Shoot plenty of pictures while you're waiting and stalking, but try not to think of the outcome, or final pictures. Think of the shutter clicks only as clicks and as a part of <u>now</u>. If you start thinking ahead to prints or slides you will get and print (PV? Here the actor has shifted to an orientation to the situation of taking pictures of cats, and relates that to the orientation toward the cat), the quiet drama may drain from dynamic waiting and turn it into a chore. You may be helped in this if before shooting, you decide to delay a month or two in processing your film. (PV?) Just wrap it in foil and pop it into the icebox to preserve the image quality.

Take another tip from the cat's book: don't combine waiting with regret for what you did not do or opportunities missed when the cat did something special. (PVs?) Dynamic waiting is a now thing, but regret is hanging on to a moment past. And while you're regretting a picture you've missed, three more will pass by without your seeing them. Clinging to regret is also a way of badly underestimating your cat, like thinking he's already done everything interesting (PV?) he is likely to do in a lifetime.

You should approach your cat with respect. (PVs?) The fact is that he has nothing to learn from you that will improve his ability to be more fully a cat. But you can learn much from him by thinking about his pure "beingness". (PV?) By studying him you can learn about a being that is entirely alien to man, but that is a completed universe, not a fragmented, egocentric entity like man. And then you'll probably learn to love him for what he is -- a cat. (PV?)

ANALYSIS:

1. Look back over the margin notes you have made, distinguishing between what the photographer thinks should be the correct orientation of an actor toward the photography of a cat, and what it should not be. Try to "sum up" what you have found, and fill in the chart below:

SHOULD USE

AFF			AFF NEUT
UNIV			PART
QUAL			PERF
SPEC			DIFF

SHOULD NOT USE

AFF			AFF NEUT
UNIV			PART
QUAL			PERF
SPEC			DIFF

2. Look at the sets of Pattern Variables under the Should (what the actor thinks is the right way to be oriented toward photographing cats) and Should Not categories. What is the "general" Phase emphasis? You may find some slight inconsistencies, but do you find an overall Phase direction, and what is it?

SHOULD USE

A	
G	
I	
L	

SHOULD NOT USE

A	
G	
I	
L	

3. What is the Phase emphasized, and what is the Phase rejected?

4. Using Plate V, decide what Functional Imperative you would expect to find with the role of photographer.

What did you find?

5. What is the general significance of this little essay on cats for American Society in general?

APPLICATION IV
CREATING A NEW GAME

Many people think that American games, such as football, baseball, basketball, bridge, Monoply, etc. are too competitive and "Adaptive Phase". As a result, there is a rise of interest in "New Games" where there is a conscious effort to reject those Pattern Variable orientations.

A. Design a game that is L Phase or I Phase in its orientation. Explain what your rules will be and how the game is to be played.

B. Explain how your game reflects each of the Pattern Variables of the Phase you have chosen.

APPLICATION V
JONATHAN LIVINGSTON SEAGULL

This book by Richard Bach has appealed to many Americans. Using the General Theory of Action, analyze what Bach is rejecting and what he is suggesting as a mode of orientation toward the world. What is Jonathan teaching? (Do not get WHAT is taught mixed up with HOW it is taught.) What are the values represented by the goals and what Pattern Variable orientations should be used in attempting to achieve those valued goals or states? How is "love" defined? How does one go about learning to "love?" (Be careful to distinguish between the word "love" and Parsons' translation of it, and Bach's translation of its meaning.)

You may want to use the following format:

ACTOR	ORIENTATIONS	GOALS
Jon	Culture System Social System	Flying Love

APPLICATION VI
OTHER BOOKS

The following books and articles are also recommended for anaysis using the General Theory of Action:

Dorothy M. Johnson. "A Man Called Horse" in INDIAN COUNTRY by Dorothy M. Johnson. McIntosh and Otis, Inc., 1949, reprinted from COLLIER'S.

Ken Kesey, ONE FLEW OVER THE CUCKOO'S NEST. New York: New American Library, 1962.

B.F. Skinner. WALDEN TWO. New York: The Macmillan Co. 1948.

Robert Heinlein, THE MOON IS A HARSH MISTRESS. New York: G.P. Putnam, 1966.

Tom Wolfe, THE RIGHT STUFF. New York: Farrar, Straus, Giroux, 1979.

Robert M. Pirsig. ZEN AND THE ART OF MOTORCYCLE MAINTENANCE. New York: William Morrow Bantam Book, 1974.

Richard Adams. WATERSHIP DOWN. New York: Macmillan Publishing Co Avon Books, 1972.

Robert Sheckley. CAN YOU FEEL ANYTHING WHEN I DO THIS? New York: Daw Books, 1961. (A book of essays.)

Roseabeth Moss Kanter: COMMITMENT AND COMMUNITY: COMMUNES AND UTOPIAS IN SOCIOLOGICAL PERSPECTIVE. Cambridge, MA: Harvard University Press, 1972. (An interesting use of some of the aspects of the General Theory of Action without the terminiology.)

APPLICATION VII
THE AMERICAN EDUCATIONAL SYSTEM

There is a lot of criticism of the American educational system recently. Using the General Theory of Action, examine how the American educational system works and how and if it fulfills the Latent Pattern Maintenance Functional Imperatives. You might want to take your college catalogue and find the statement of purpose and goals of the institution, and then compare that with the requirements for graduation. (A comparision of Culture System and Social System levels.) You know the expected Pattern Variables, etc. which should be found in the L Phase as that is where primary socialization falls in the Functional Imperatives. Consider how Spilldown from the Adaptive Phase could be effecting the systems of grading, funding, and teacher evaluation for example. Show where the system does and does not work. In those areas where you think it is not fulfilling the Functional Imperatives, devise a plan that would.

APPLICATION VIII
NOT ENOUGH
PATTERN VARIABLE COMBINATIONS?
(Very Difficult)

Perhaps the General Theory of Action is not complex enough. Look carefully at the Integrative Phase Pattern Variables which fulfill functions of social control through enforcement and legislation. Also examine the expanded Pattern Variable combinations on pp. 250 and 252 of TOWARD A GENERAL THEORY OF ACTION. What other Pattern Variable combinations might be used in this Phase? How would they improve the analytical ability of the theory? Or, do you think this view that the Integrative Pattern Variables are not complete is simply an effect of "Spilldown" from the Adaptive Phase?

APPENDIX
SUPPLEMENTAL READINGS

I. Intellectual History of the General Theory of Action

THE STRUCTURE OF SOCIAL ACTION. Talcott Parsons. VOL I & II. New York: The Free Press. 1968.

II. Theory in General

TOWARD A GENERAL THEORY OF ACTION, Parsons and Shils, Eds. Cambridge, MA: Harvard University Press. 1959. pp. 3-41; 47-51; 61-64.

CONCEPTS, THEORY, AND EXPLANATION IN THE BEHAVIORAL SCIENCES. Gordon DiRenzo, ed. New York: Random House. 1966. pp. 21-40.

THE STRUCTURE OF SOCIAL ACTION, Vol I, Talcott Parsons. New York: The Free Press. 1968. pp. 3-42.

III. Elements of Action

TOWARD A GENERAL THEORY OF ACTION, Parsons and Shils. pp. 4-27; 53-60; 64-76; 98-123.

IV. Sub-Systems of Action

TOWARD A GENERAL THEORY OF ACTION, Parsons and Shils. pp. 190-230; 110-158; 159;189.

THE SOCIAL SYSTEM, Talcott Parsons. Glencoe, IL: The Free Press. 1951.

SOCIAL STRUCTURE AND PERSONALITY, Talcott Parsons. New York: The Free Press of Glencoe. 1964.

V. The System of Action

TOWARD A GENERAL THEORY OF ACTION, Parsons and Shils. pp. 177, 241.

THE SOCIAL SYSTEM, Talcott Parsons. pp. 26-36.

VI. The Pattern Variables

TOWARD A GENERAL THEORY OF ACTION, Parsons and Shils. pp. 76-98

"Pattern Variables Revisited: A Response to Robert Dubin". Talcott Parsons. AMERICAN SOCIOLOGICAL REVIEW, Vol. 25, No. 4 (August, 1960).

VII. Essays, and Other Applications

ESSAYS IN SOCIOLOGICAL THEORY, Talcott Parsons, rev. ed. Glencoe, IL: The Free Press. 1954.

SOCIOLOGICAL THEORY AND MODERN SOCIETY, Talcott Parsons. New York: The Free Press. 1967.

SOCIAL SYSTEMS AND THE EVOLUTION OF ACTION THEORY, Talcott Parsons. New York: The Free Press. 1977.

ECONOMY AND SOCIETY: A STUDY IN THE INTEGRATION OF ECONOMIC AND SOCIAL THEORY. Talcott Parsons and Neil Smelser. Glencoe, IL: The Free Press. 1956.

STRUCTURE AND PROCESS IN MODERN SOCIETIES, Talcott Parsons. Glencoe, IL: The Free Press. 1960.

VIII. Change and Evolution

SOCIETIES: EVOLUTIONARY AND COMPARATIVE PERSPECTIVES. Talcott Parsons. Englewood Cliffs, N.J.: Prentice-Hall. 1966.

THE EVOLUTION OF SOCIETIES. Talcott Parsons. Englewood Cliffs, N.J.: Prentice-Hall. 1977.

IX. Complete Bibliography and Essays

ACTION THEORY AND THE HUMAN CONDITION. Talcott Parsons. New York: The Free Press. 1978.

FOOTNOTES

1. Max Weber. "'Objectivity' in Social Science and Social Policy" in Maurice Natanson, Ed. PHILOSOPHY OF THE SOCIAL SCIENCES: A READER. New York: Random House, 1963, p. 417.
2. Charles Ackerman and Talcott Parsons. "The Concept of 'Social System' as a Theoretical Device" in Gordon J. DiReinzo, CONCEPTS, THEORY, AND EXPLANATION IN THE BEHAVIORAL SCIENCES. New York: Random House, 1966. See pp. 24-27 for this entire quotation.
3. Talcott Parsons. THE STRUCTURE OF SOCIAL ACTION, VOL I. New York: The Free Press, 1968, p. 41.
4. Stuart Chase. THE TYRANNY OF WORDS. New York: Harcourt, Brace & Co., p. 33.
5. Ackerman and Parsons, OP. CIT., p. 41.
6. Talcott Parsons. THE STRUCTURE OF SOCIAL ACTION, VOL I. New York: The Free Press, 1968. p.8.
7. Ackerman and Parsons, OP. CIT., P. 32.
8. IBID., p. 31.
9. Talcott Parsons. SOCIOLOGICAL THEORY AND MODERN SOCIETY. New York: The Free Press. 1967. p. 225.
10. Talcott Parsons. "Death in American Society". Lecture Manuscript of a talk given at the University of California at Los Angeles, 1964. Published in THE AMERICAN BEHAVIORAL SCIENTIST (May) 1963.
11. Talcott Parsons, SOCIOLOGICAL THEORY AND MODERN SOCIETY. OP. CIT., pp. 385-421.
12. Talcott Parsons. ESSAYS IN SOCIOLOGICAL THEORY. Rev. Ed. Glencoe, IL: The Free Press. 1954. pp. 104-123.

INDEX

The General Theory of Action

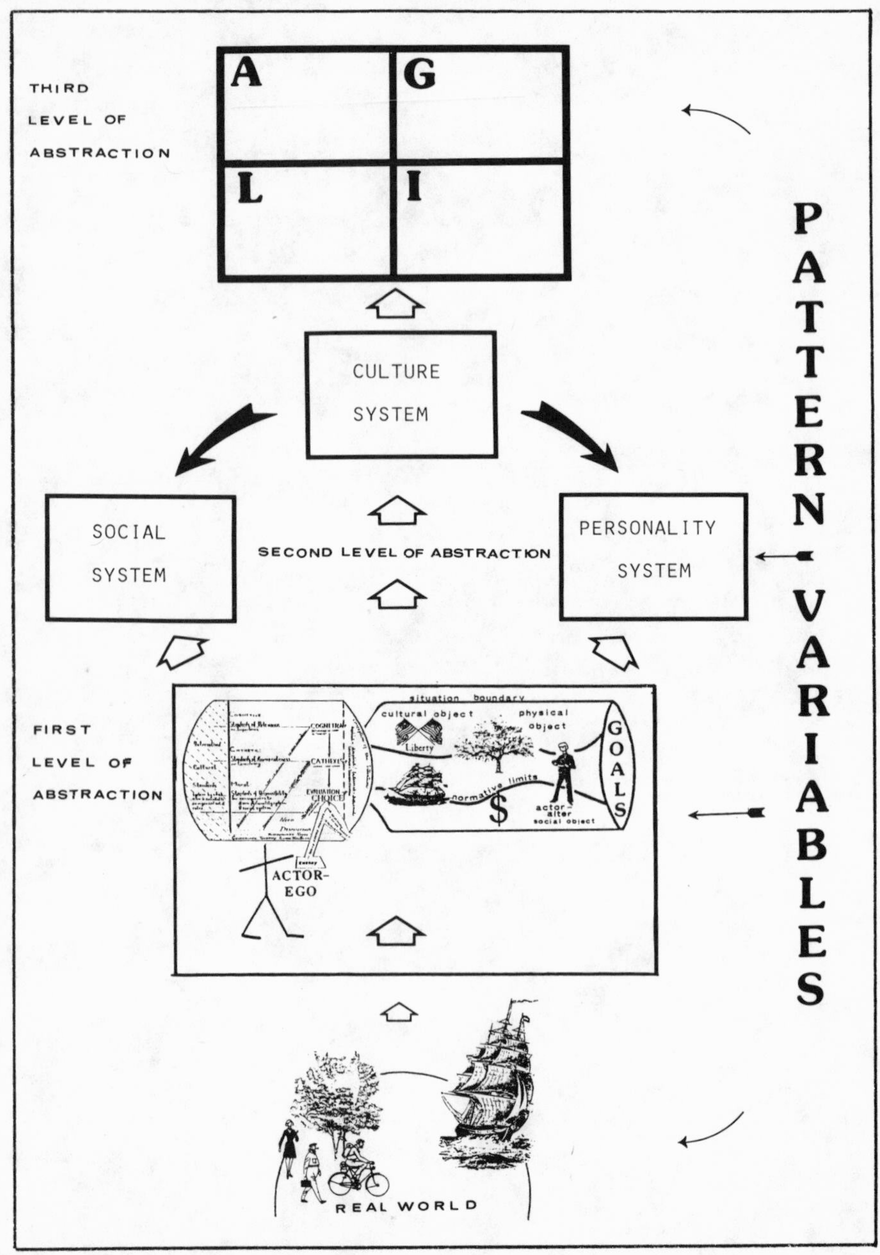

THE ELEMENTS OF ACTION

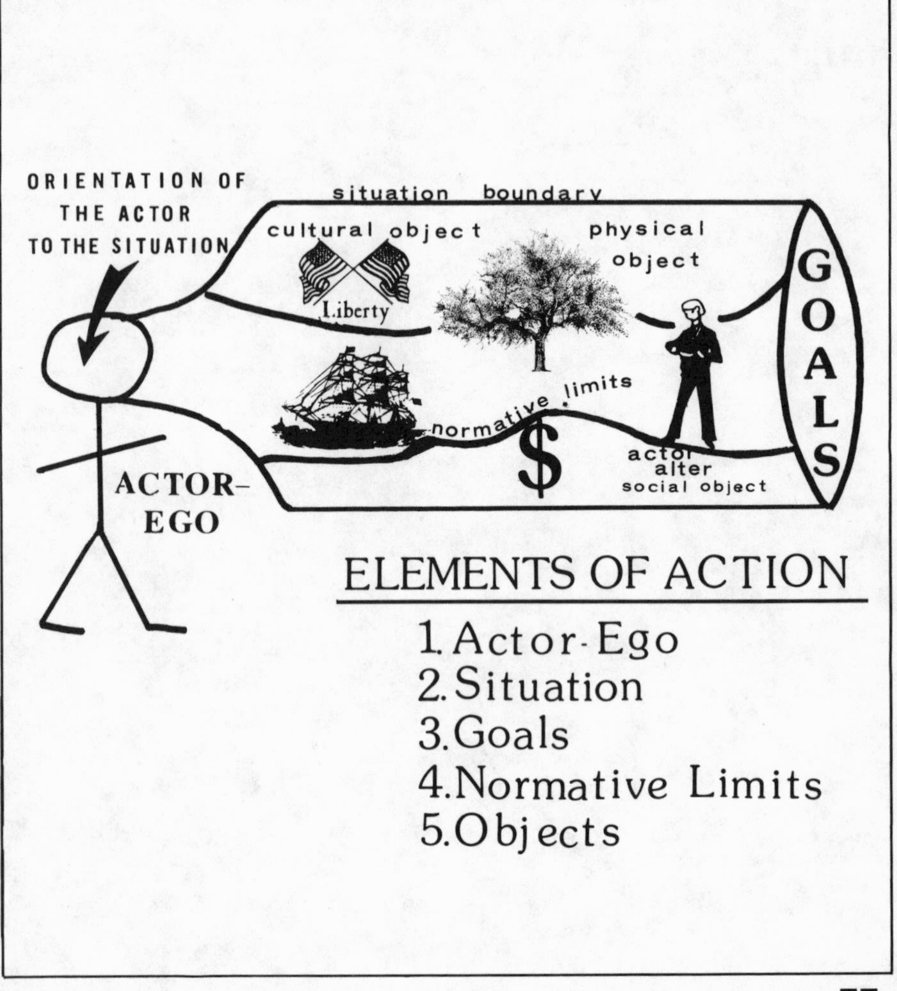

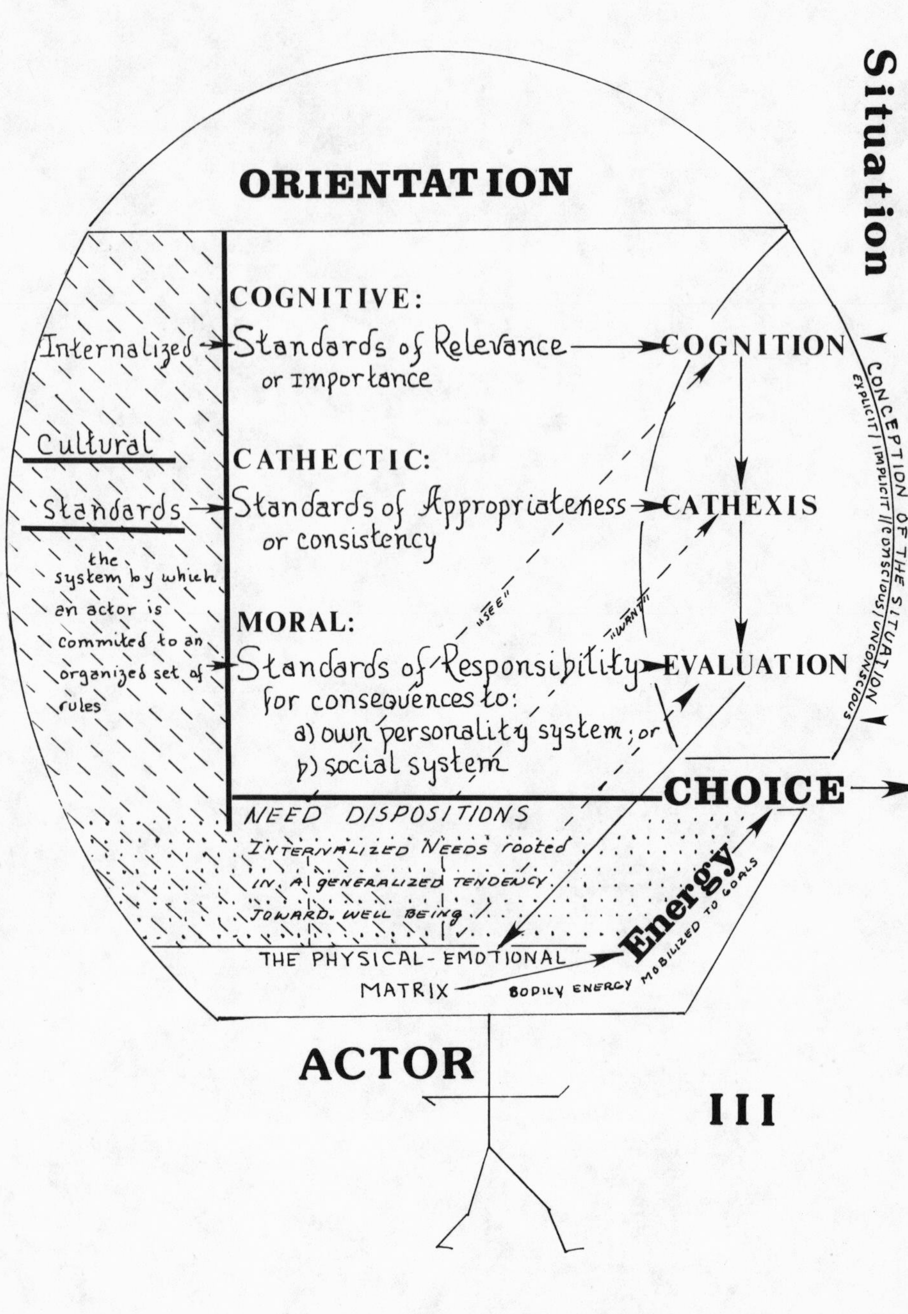

ORIENTATION
Situation
COGNITIVE:
Internalized
Standards of Relevance
or importance
COGNITION
Cultural
Standards
the system by which an actor is commited to an organized set of rules
CATHECTIC:
Standards of Appropriateness
or consistency
CATHEXIS
CONCEPTION OF THE SITUATION
EXPLICIT / IMPLICIT // CONSCIOUS / UNCONSCIOUS
MORAL:
"SEE"
"WANT"
Standards of Responsibility
for consequences to:
a) own personality system; or
b) social system
EVALUATION
CHOICE
NEED DISPOSITIONS
INTERNALIZED NEEDS rooted
IN A GENERALIZED TENDENCY
TOWARD WELL BEING
Energy
MOBILIZED TO GOALS
THE PHYSICAL-EMOTIONAL
MATRIX
BODILY ENERGY
ACTOR
III